THE EVER-CHANGING COASTLINE

Tidal Forces at Work

JOSEPH R. VOTANO

4880 Lower Valley Road · Atglen, PA 19310

Other Schiffer Books by Joseph R. Votano:
The Timeless Seashore, ISBN 978-0-7643-5488-5

Other Schiffer Books on Related Subjects:
The Cape Cod National Seashore: A Photographic Adventure & Guide, Christopher Seufert, ISBN 978-0-7643-3995-0

Lighthouses and Coastal Attractions of Southern New England: New Hampshire, Maine, and Vermont, Allan Wood, ISBN 978-0-7643-5245-4

Lighthouses and Coastal Attractions of Northern New England: Connecticut, Rhode Island, and Massachusetts, Allan Wood, ISBN 978-0-7643-5235-5

Library of Congress Control Number: 2017953844

Designed by Brenda McCallum
Type set in Aldine401/ Bernhard Tango

ISBN: 978-0-7643-5487-8

Printed in China

Published by Schiffer Publishing, Ltd.
4880 Lower Valley Road | Atglen, PA 19310
Phone: (610) 593-1777; Fax: (610) 593-2002
E-mail: Info@schifferbooks.com
Web: www.schifferbooks.com

CONTENTS

Acknowledgments

I'd like to thank the designers and editors at Schiffer Publishing for their work on this book, as well as Karen Hosking, Karl Schanz, Ken Jordan, and Robert Lamacq, who contributed various images. Most of all, thank you to my wife, Gail, whose patience and support made this book possible.

Introduction

Nothing in nature is more dynamic than the seashore, with its endless tides, shifting sands, ocean currents, and the sound of waves rhythmically washing the shore. Anyone who has spent time by the ocean never forgets its infinite expanse and the sense of solitude and relaxation it brings. Tidal forces, a result of the sun and moon's gravitational pull, create mysterious landforms such as cliffs, chasms, sandbars, and sea stacks, which are formed by the energy of the ocean acting on headlands.

The joy of being at the seashore is a lasting memory for most of us. Forty percent of the world's population (approximately 2.9 billion people) live within thirty-seven miles of the sea, and roughly half the world's populations derive food sources from the oceans. Humans, too, leave their footprint on the seashore with harbors, piers, boats, and lighthouses.

The images in this book attempt to bring to life the most striking scenes that I and a several other photographers have come across in North America and elsewhere. Whether it is a foggy day on the Maine coast, reflections from a rolling wave, a fiery sunset along the Oregon coast, or a towering lighthouse, I hope these images give readers a greater appreciation for oceans and their seashores. They are, after all, wondrous.

Beaches, Tides, Waves & Sea Stacks

BEACHES

Beaches change every day due to the continual action of tides, waves, winds, and ocean currents, which move sand, gravel, rocks, and vegetation from place to place. As the sea level rises, beaches also move inland, altering the landscape. Every beach is a product of its composition of sand and/or gravel, wave energy, tidal currents, and sea level. These factors are in dynamic equilibrium, and when one changes, the others are altered. Various combinations of these elements lead to different types of beaches. The major types of beaches are barrier island, mainland, pocket, and cape. Excluding human activity, the sand, gravel, and rocks come from a variety of principal sources: cliff erosion, adjacent beaches, rock weathering (chemical and physical), glaciers, the seabed, and rivers. Such source differences give rise to grains of sand that differ in size, color, shape, mineralogical composition, and density. Some beaches have very fine sand; others have coarse grains. Some beaches are covered with a variety of rocks, from tiny granules to large boulders. Retreating glaciers in the higher northern altitudes (above 40°) left behind boulders, pebbles, and cobblestones one finds on beaches and along shorelines in New England and Eastern Canada (see Appendix).

The most common mineral in sand is quartz (see Appendix), which is responsible for white beaches like Clearwater Beach in Florida (**Plate 1**). Quartz is found in igneous, sedimentary, and metamorphic rocks. The second most common grain minerals are carbonates (i.e., calcium carbonate, $CaCO_3$) in the form of limestone reduced to sand via physical abrasion and/or erosion. The next most abundant minerals are the feldspars, which are aluminum silicates. Most beaches are not white but various shades of tan ranging from reddish color to yellowish-brown in color (**Plates 2–4, 6),** while others are grayish (**Plates 5** and **7**). Iron oxide stains quartz, feldspar, and shell fragments to varying degrees—hence the varying shades of beach sand.

Another type of beach material, found mostly in warm climates, is made up of calcareous materials (finely ground seashells and/or coral). Calcareous beaches are mainly composed of calcium carbonate as a result of storm-wave action that strips barnacles, mussels, and urchins off rocks and then grinds them to sand-sized grains. There are a few such beaches in the northeastern United States, one of which is Sand Beach in Acadia National Park in Maine. It's a pocket beach wedged between two headlands (**Plate 8**). Instead of being whitish-gray, it's a light tan color, probably due to iron oxide staining.

PLATE | 1 |

PLATE | 2 |

PLATE | 3 |

PLATE | 4 |

PLATE | 5 |

PLATE | 6 |

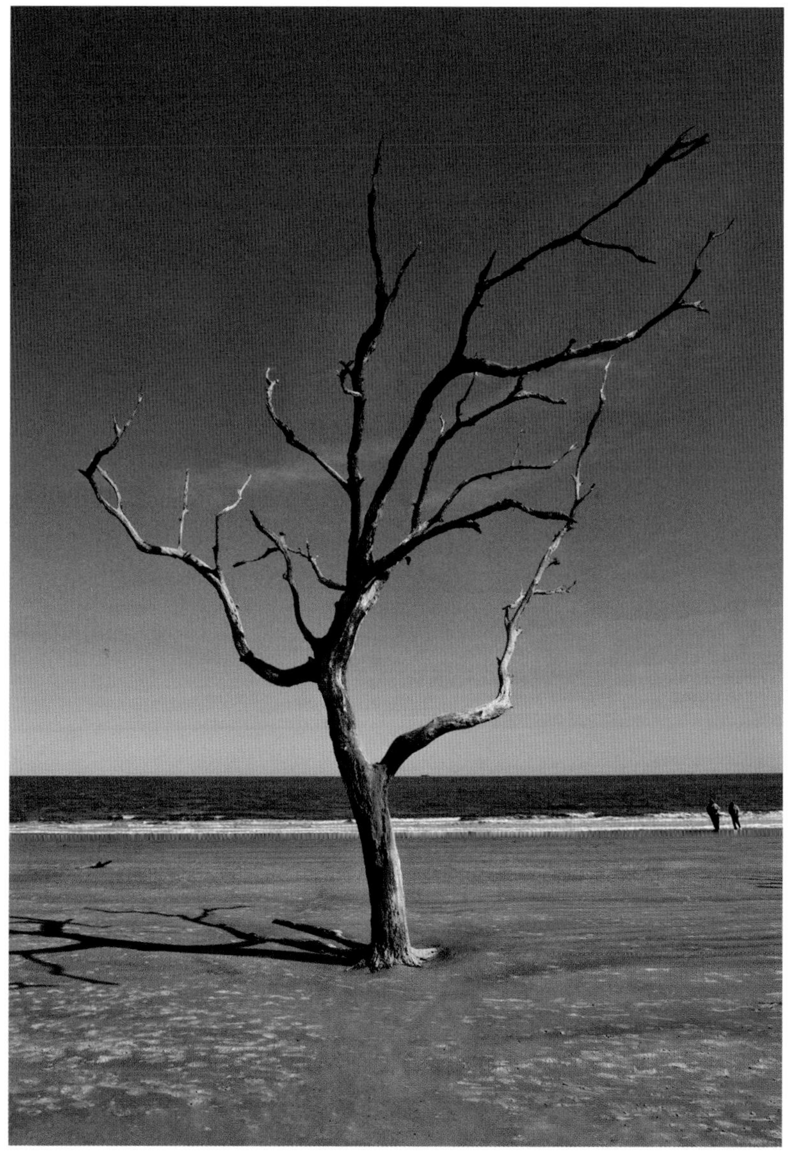

PLATE | 7 |

Plate 7 was taken at Driftwood Beach on Jekyll Island, Georgia. The dead tree is an oddity: first, because it is still standing; and second, because it is all by itself. The beach is hard-packed sand and littered with downed trees with their sprawling root systems. Then there is this puzzling, stand-alone tree.

PLATE | 8 |

15

TIDES

> The three great elemental sounds in nature are the sounds of rain, the sound of the wind, and the sound of the outer ocean on a beach. I have heard them all and that of the ocean is the most awesome, beautiful, and varied.
> — *Henry Beston*

Beaches are the most dynamic places on Earth, and central to this dynamism are the tides. Tides, waves, winds, and coastal geometries above and below the water determine where tides end up on a beach, the height of the waves, and the energy contained in waves. All these factors work together to sculpt a beach, second-by-second.

The gravitational pull of the moon, and to a lesser extent the sun, causes a daily rise and fall of ocean tides. Most common are the semidiurnal tides (twice a day tides): high to low to high again over a 12.25-hour period. With the Earth spinning at 1,037 mph (1670 km/h) about its axis, there are two high and low tides per day. Oceans nearest the moon experience a bulge, or inbound acceleration, as the Earth is drawn slightly toward the moon, while the ocean waters farthest from the moon recede. Tides change in height over the twenty-eight-day lunar cycle. At a new or full moon, the spring tides are the highest (see Fig. A). Here the moon and sun are pulling in the same direction. At a 90-degree position between sun and moon (see Fig. B), the neap tide occurs—the lowest tide in the lunar cycle. During the month, of course, tide heights vary from day to day, and the time of high or low tide advances by fifty minutes each day.

Spring Tide

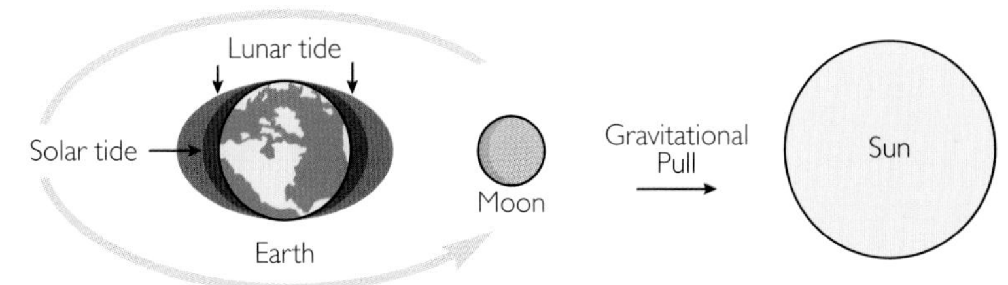

FIGURE | A |

Neap Tide

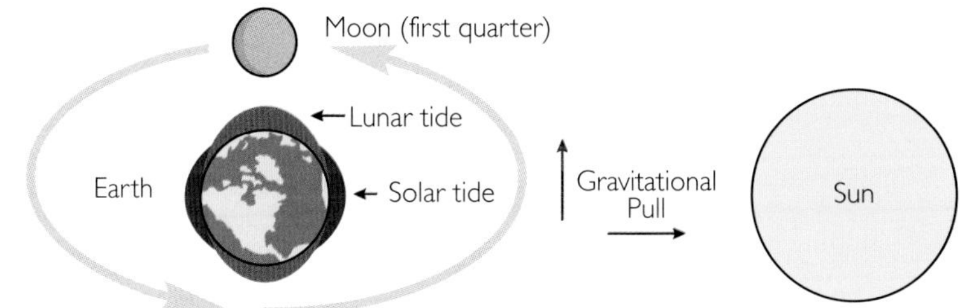

FIGURE | B |

Bay of Fundy, between New Brunswick and Nova Scotia in Canada, has the highest tidal range at 42 feet (12.8 m) to 47.5 feet (14.5 m)—see **Plate 9** of the bay at Hopewell, New Brunswick. Another high tidal range is at Mont Saint Michel Bay, (190 square miles/500 km^{2}in area), located between southwest Brittany and the Normandy peninsula. The tidal range is in excess of 32 feet (~10 m). **Plate 10** gives a long view of this bay taken from Mont Saint-Michel Abbey as the tide was rolling in under a fog bank.

PLATE | 9 |

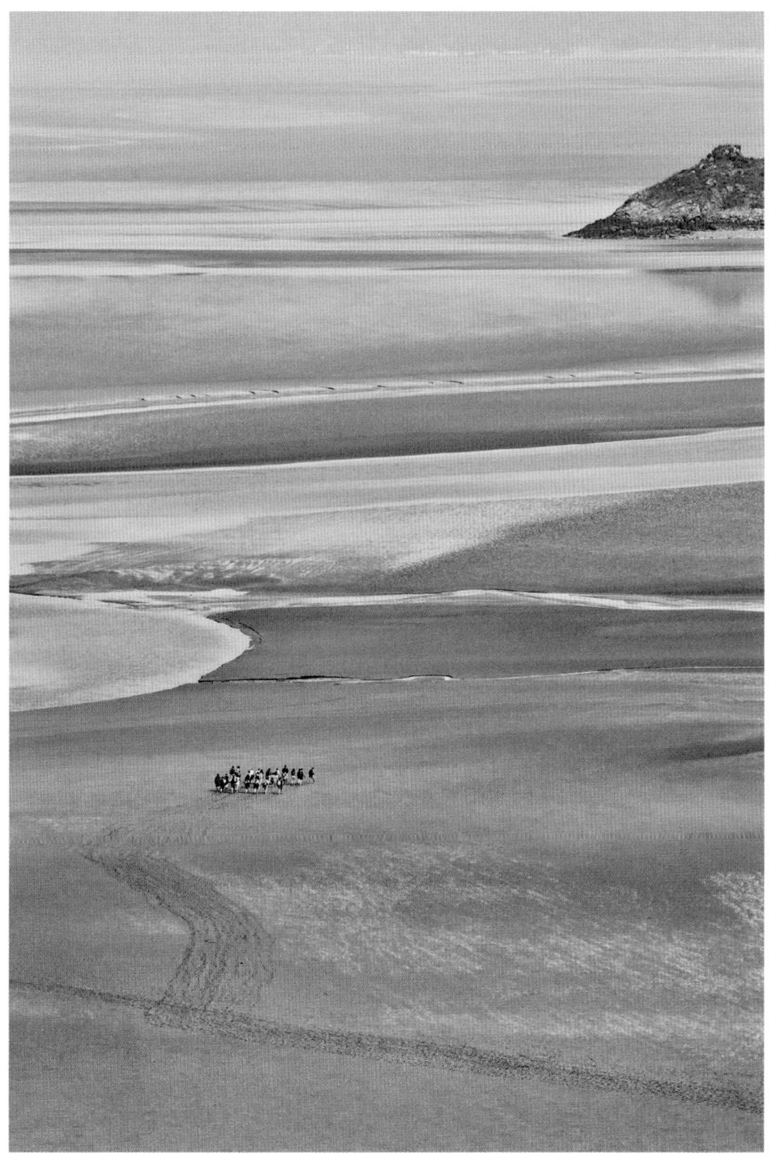

PLATE | 10 |

WAVES

Waves are the most important force determining the structure and composition of a beach. The energy contained in waves allows them to carry sediment, to move and sort small rocks and grains of sand, and to change the shape of a beach. In the open ocean, the energy housed in a wave is proportional to the square of the wave height (Fig. C), the distance from trough to crest.

Winds blowing across the ocean surface impart their energy to the water via surface friction. The waveform then moves the energy (not the water) toward the beach. Think of snapping a rope. The energy travels down the rope but doesn't move it forward. This phenomenon approximates what happens with ocean waves where stronger winds result in bigger waves with greater energy and weaker winds results in smaller waves with less energy. Waves due to storms in the open sea can surpass 50 feet (greater than 12 m) in height, while swell waves due to storms close to shore can reach, on average, 3 feet (1 m). Waves in the Atlantic Ocean range in height from 2 feet to 7 feet (0.05–2.1 m),while those in the Pacific Ocean average 11 feet (3.4 m); 10 percent are 22 feet (6.7 m) high. Storms just offshore can set up waves similar to what happens far offshore. Anyone witnessing a hurricane along the eastern seaboard of the US can attest to waves that wash whole shorelines out to sea.

Waves coming from an open ocean create various water conditions along the shoreline. As waves approach the shoreline with its shallower waters, they start to interact with the seabed. When the wave steepness, defined as ratio of wavelength to wave height (Fig. C), reaches a value around 7, the wave becomes unstable and starts to crumble. A plunging breaker wave creates the commonly seen white caps.

Beaches with a gentle underwater slope usually have waves that break far from the shoreline and come gently ashore. Another type of wave is called a surging breaker. These waves rush up a beach without breaking, and all their energy is dissipated on a reflective surface, e.g., a steep graveled slope or a physical surface. **Plate 11** shows an example of a surging breaker wave hitting a partially convex-shaped concrete wall. All its energy is used to throw up tons of water approximately 25 feet into the air.

The Wave

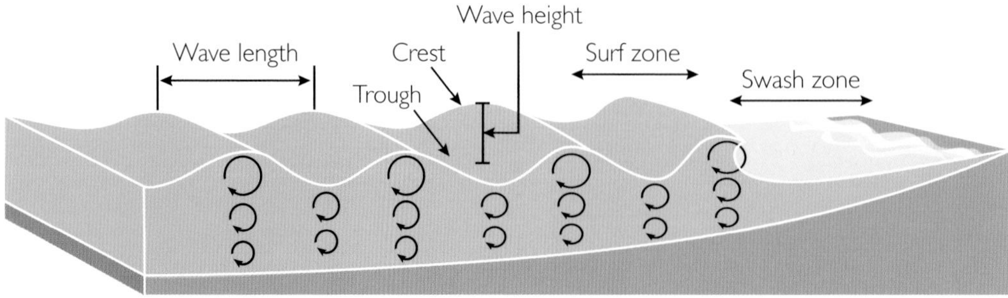

FIGURE | C |

PLATE | 11 |

SEA STACKS

Like inanimate sentinels, sea stacks rise up from the ocean floor to create striking forms. They can take on many shapes: some are straight columns, others are humped, while some are twisted and hollowed out at their base by continuous erosion from wave action. Sea stacks are found off many coastal headlands from Victoria in Australia, to Phang Nga Bay in Thailand, to the Parus Rock in the Black Sea, to Hoy Island in the Orkney Island chain off the Scottish coast, to the volcanic Ball's Pyramid far from land in the Pacific Ocean, and to the beaches in the US Northwest.

Unprotected headlands that jut out into the sea are the most likely conditions for sea stack formations. First ocean waves chisel away at the internal cracks, accompanied by wind carrying sand, which further cuts into the rock over time. Then physical and thermal stresses act on the exposed rock surfaces to deepen the cracks. Eventually rock pieces fall away to form one or more caves. Continued pounding, especially during storms with their large ocean swells, causes cave walls to give way; then the water bores straight through the remaining thin walls, forming an arch (Fig. D). With more pounding, the arch continues to grow until it breaks away from the mainland as Earth above the arch comes crashing down due to lack of support.

The coastal headlands of Oregon and Washington have many sea stack formations. Bandon Beach in Southwestern Oregon is simply loaded with eye-catching stacks and land masses (see **Plates 12–16**).

Sea stacks are fascinating in their variety of sizes, shapes, locations, and degree of erosion. **Plates 13**, **15**, and **16** illustrate the distances from shore of the trapezoidal and triangular-shaped stacks. Shore to stack distances can easily run 200 yards (183 m) or more, which translates to an immense amount of headland erosion. Particles from this erosion likely make up some of the sand in coastal beaches. Seal Rock Beach, ten miles south of Newport, Oregon, is unique (**Plate 17**). The first thing one notices is a series of pocket beaches lining the shore. The line of stacks runs parallel to the headland for some distance. Such an alignment is quite rare.

Formation of a Stack

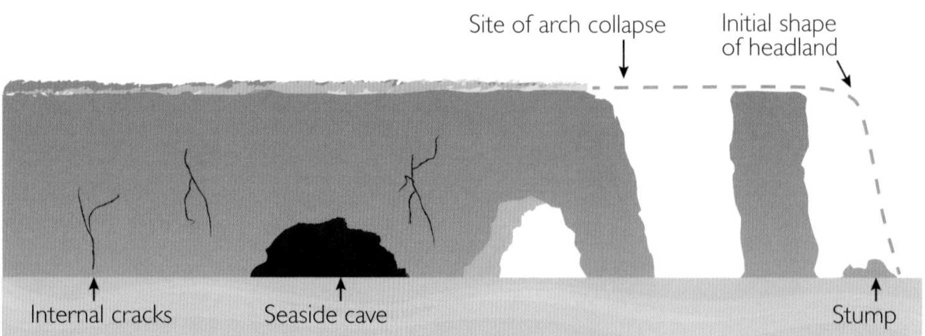

FIGURE | D |

Plate 19 shows two stacks at Hopewell Rocks in New Brunswick, Canada, on the Bay of Fundy. The dark-colored stacks are composed of sedimentary and sandstone rock and hint at the enormous heights that stacks can reach. Here, the right stack is estimated to be close to 160 feet (79 m) in height, using the person between the stacks as a guide. On the Scottish island of Hoy, a sandstone stack called the Old Man of Hoy reaches 449 feet (138 m)—just over a third of the height of the Empire State building in New York City. The volcanic Ball's Pyramid in the Pacific Ocean is 1,843 feet (568 m) tall.

PLATE | 13 |

PLATE | 14 |

PLATE | 15 |

PLATE | 16 |

PLATE | 17 |

PLATE | 18 |

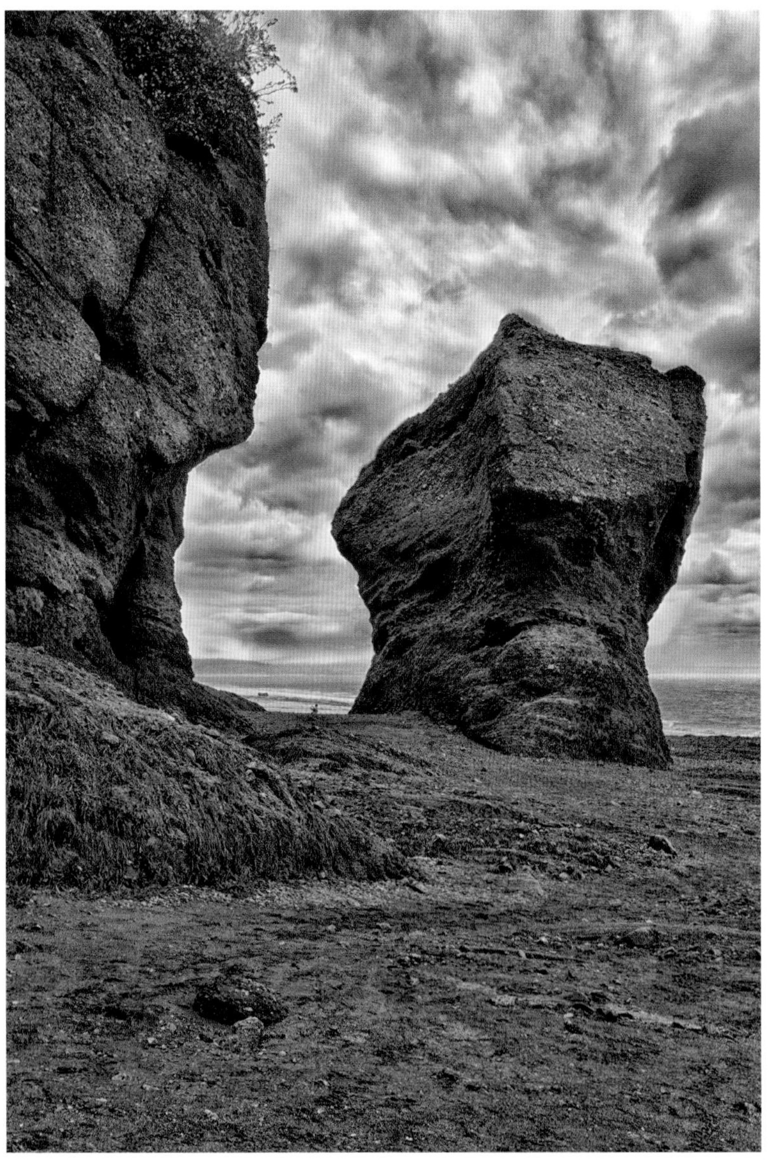

PLATE | 19 |

COASTAL DUNES & GRASSES

The formation of coastal dunes requires a supply of sand, wind, and one or more trapping mechanisms to capture blowing sand. Dune development takes place in the upper beach area, adjacent to the high-water mark. The starting dune is called a foredune. Flotsam (ship wreckage) and clumps of decaying sea vegetation brought ashore by tides can start the entrapment of blowing sand, with vegetation providing a source of nutrients for foredune plants. Next, deep-rooted, pioneering plants that are salt-tolerant take hold and start nitrogen fixation (build-up of nitrates in the sand). American and European beach grasses, called marram grasses, are the two most common plants, followed by sea oats, which are found in the Southern US, Mexico, and the Caribbean. Marram grasses grow in clusters of vertical shoots with creeping roots (rhizomes) that can extend out for yards (meters). The root system helps to anchor the plant in high winds and shifting sands, and it anchors the sand itself.

Much more so than on the Pacific coast, American beach grass along the New England coast can be found in a variety of places: covering foredunes (**Plates 20** and **24**), covering headlands high up on the beach (**Plates 21** and **22**), and covering backdunes (**Plate 31**). Grasses go from a strong, saturated green color in summer (**Plates 25–26**), to yellow in the late fall (**Plate 21**), and finally to a brownish color in the winter (**Plate 22**). If there are obstacles behind the foredune—say a rocky cliff, embankment, or road—the beach grass will grow into thick, high clusters and literally take over any remaining sand patches (see infrared images, **Plates 23** and **30**).

Other types of Atlantic coastal grasses are found in addition to the common American and European beach grasses. Marsh hay and salt marsh cordgrass are found in estuaries and creek marshes. These grasses are sometimes called salt-loving plants; in fact they are simply salt-tolerant. Marsh grass is found in estuaries composed of fine-grained sand, although, in some cases, the sand is mixed with muddy clay. Marsh hay grass usually lies above the high-tide water mark in marshes. The grass rarely reaches more than 2 feet (0.61 m) high. When the wind is blowing, the grasses look like an ocean of green waves (**Plate 27**). If that weren't enough, they turn into a sea of reddish-colored waves in the late fall (**Plate 28**)—a spectacular sight. In colonial times, the grass was fodder for livestock.

Salt marsh cordgrass is found everywhere along marsh inlets and seaward sections of marshes. Similar to beach grass, marsh cordgrass grows in upright shoots interconnected by a rhizome root system. Cordgrass can reach upward of 6 feet (1.8 m) in annual growth. Its leaves turn green in late spring and early summer, then golden by mid-October (**Plate 29**).

Winds continually reshape and move dunes farther inland. A foredune becomes a backdune once a new foredune has formed. As dunes move farther onshore, a host of new plants and trees take root in the backdune, followed by wildlife such as deer, birds, and rodents. Backdune development can be seen in two images (**Plates 30** and **31**) taken close to four years apart at almost the same location on Plum Island, a barrier island off Newburyport, Massachusetts. Although **Plate 30** is an infrared image, one still can see new growth in shrubs and small trees, and changes in the height of the background dune between October 2009 and November 2013. The sloping landform in **Plate 31** leads to a depression between the dunes called an interdunal swale. Swales are the wetland oases in dunes. They fill with water in spring, and the soil usually remains damp throughout the summer. Since the water table is close to the surface, animals can dig holes to find fresh drinking water in both summer and fall.

PLATE | 20 |

PLATE | 21 |

PLATE | 22 |

PLATE | 23 |

PLATE | 24 |

PLATE | 25 |

PLATE | 26 |

Beach grasses add rich greens and yellowish greens to the landscape throughout most of the year. Wherever there are clean, sandy beach areas (devoid of rocks) close to shore, beach grasses inevitably take over, as seen in **Plates 25** and **26**. The grasses simultaneously capture sand and slow tidal erosion. Mounds form, topped by grasses that continue to grow and spread over larger areas.

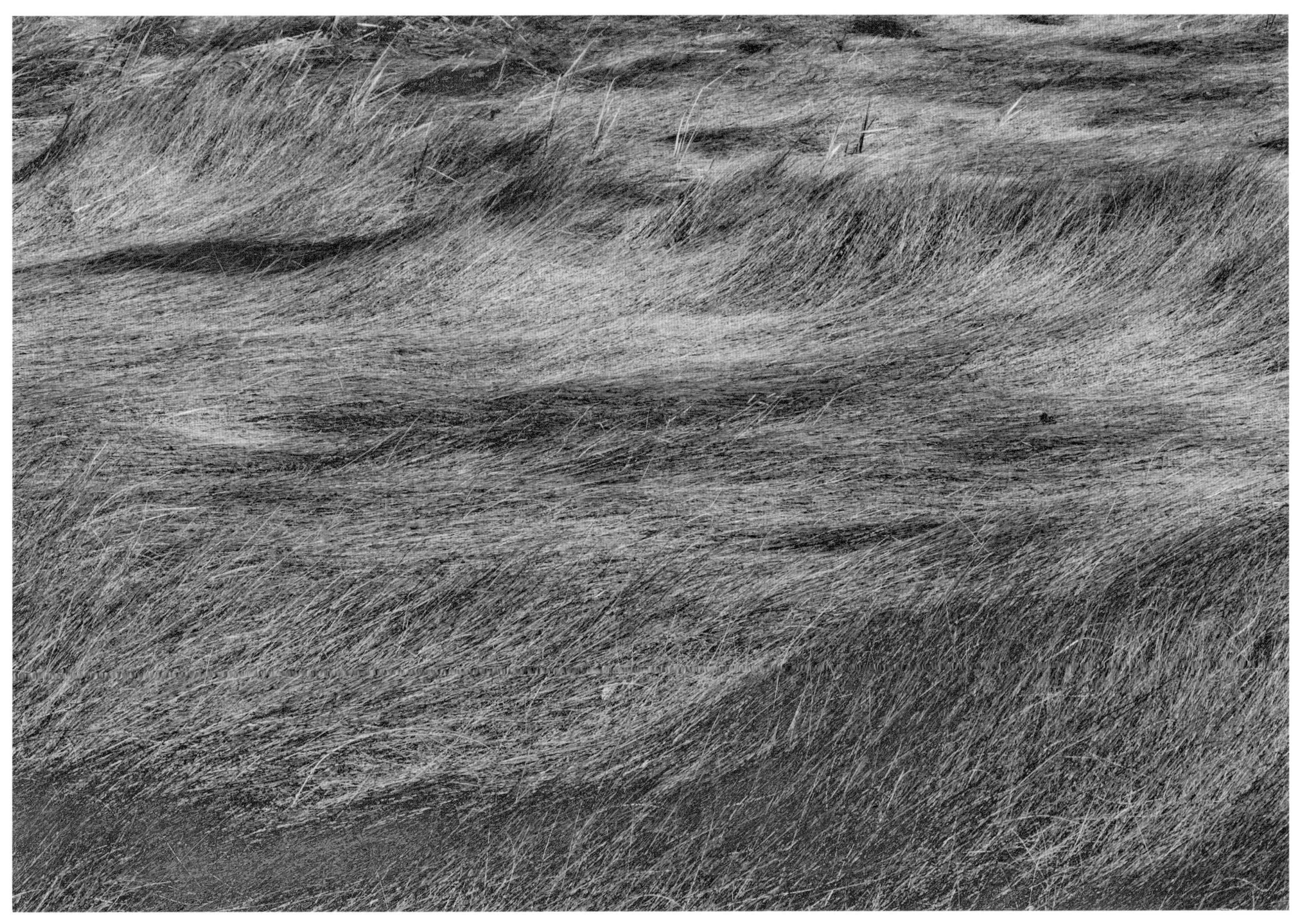

PLATE | 27 |

PLATE | 28 |

PLATE | 29 |

PLATE | 30 |

PLATE | 31 |

SEASHORE ARTISTRY

Clouds and sea, beach and wind, tides and tidal currents, and finally sand, all work together to provide continuously changing works of art. The wind is both a painter's brush and a sculptor's hand, as are the tides and ocean currents. Changing sunlight alters the hues and luminosity of colors in the shore, sea, and sky. In **Plate 32**, a lateral cloud formation seems to hover over the ocean as if put there by some unknown hand.

A tidal flow over a simple sandbar against a cloudless blue sky (**Plate 33**) created a surreal scene that will never be duplicated. The effect is so abstract that it's hard to tell what you're looking at.

When does a seascape digital image look like a painting? Well, there is no easy answer to this question since there is a whole group of photo-realistic painters who create paintings that look like photographs. But perhaps the answer is quite simple: when it looks like a painting. **Plate 34** is such an image. It's a fifteen-second exposure taken just after sunrise in heavy cloud cover, shooting downward from a headland on Cape Cod Bay; the soft-focus effect, due to a long exposure, gives it a painterly look. It might have been done by Georgia O'Keeffe, given its simplicity, composition, and pastel colors.

Plate 35 also looks like a painting. It's a twenty-second exposure on a cloudy day using a 10x neutral density filter to achieve the long exposure. Waves break parallel to the shore because of submerged sandbars just offshore, which are captured as light and dark rows.

Every beach has unique surface characteristics, however large or small, due to different sedimentary structures or bedforms that alter the smooth surface of a tidal flat. These bedforms can be formed in hours, minutes, or even seconds by changes in wind, sand, waves, and tidal and longshore currents. Sand ripples, or ripple marks, are the most common type of surface structures on tidal flats. There are dozens of different types of ripple marks and names to go with their shapes. A few are seen in **Plates 36**, **38**, and **41**. Ladder-back ripples are shown in **Plate 36**. They are produced by one set of ripples superimposed at 90 degrees onto a second set; this gives the appearance of ladder rungs. **Plate 37** is an example of near-shore ripples, shown here to the right of the human footprints. They are normally asymmetric with low amplitude (crest height). The largest ripple marks are appropriately named megaripples (**Plate 38**), which are formed by strong wave or tidal currents. Smaller ripples cover the megaripples to give a somewhat distorted appearance. Megaripples have small, dune-like features with crest spacing running from 2–20 feet (0.6–6 m) and amplitudes between 4 and 20 inches (10–50 cm).

To understand the artistry imprinted on beaches, we have to understand the effect of water and air and how tides and currents transport and mold sand. We start with the empty spaces between packed sand grains known as the void or pore volume. The value of the void volume is called the porosity of the sand, which can range from 20 percent to 50 percent. Air fills this void volume first as the tide goes out and then with water when the tide comes in. Water to fill the voids can come not just from ocean waves crashing over the beach, but also from land drainage in non-arid climates. The water table under the beach rises up with a rising tide, which, in turn, saturates the sand above the water table. In a falling tide, the water level falls, and with it, the water flows seaward out of the void space, resulting in surface water seepage, a common sight at low tide. This seaward flow creates rill marks that carve out dendritic (tree-like) patterns (**Plates 39–41**). The sculpted patterns look like river deltas viewed from above.

PLATE | 32 |

PLATE | 33 |

PLATE | 34 |

PLATE | 35 |

PLATE | 36 |

PLATE | 37 |

PLATE | 38 |

PLATE | 39 |

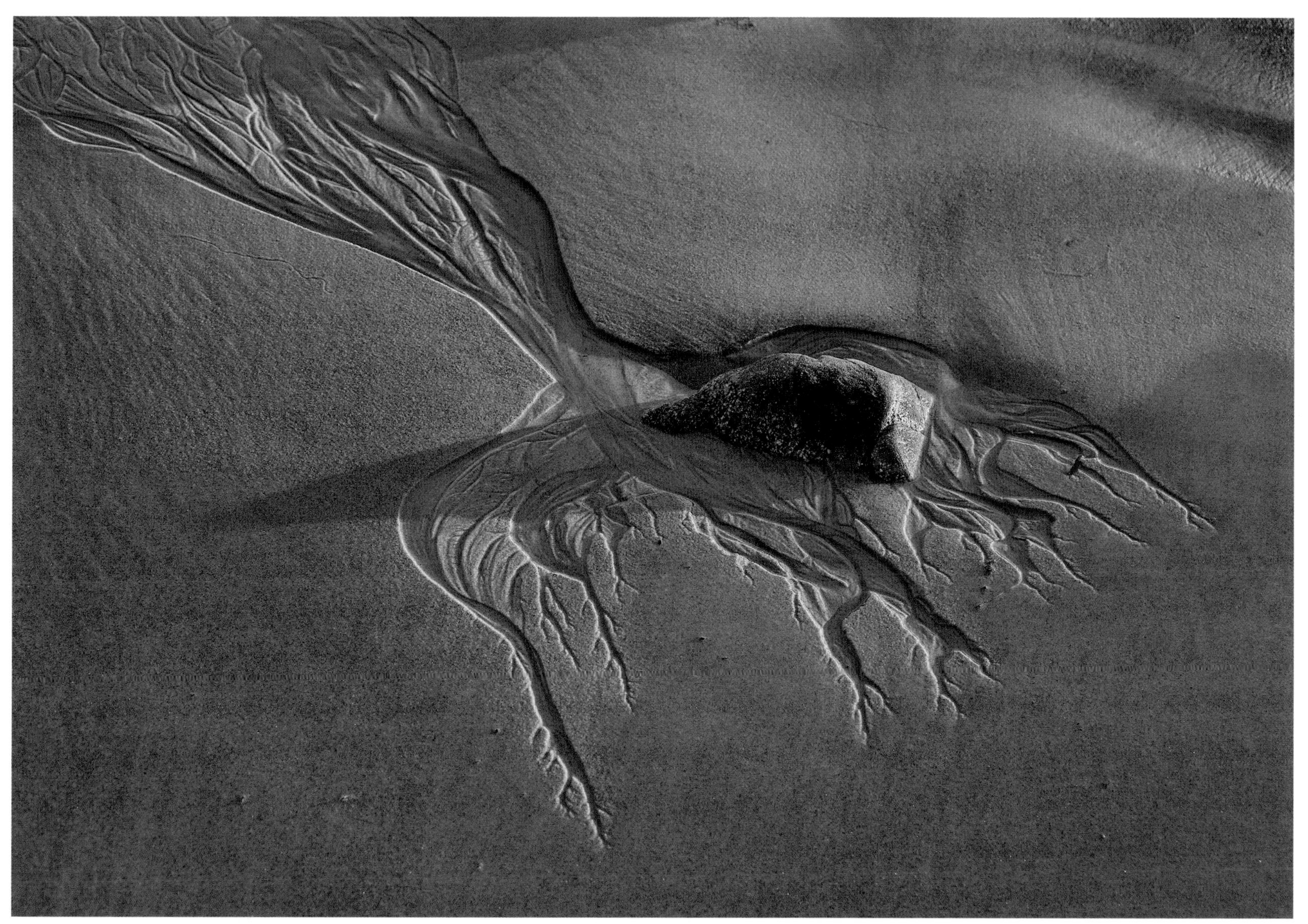

PLATE | 40 |

PLATE | 41 |

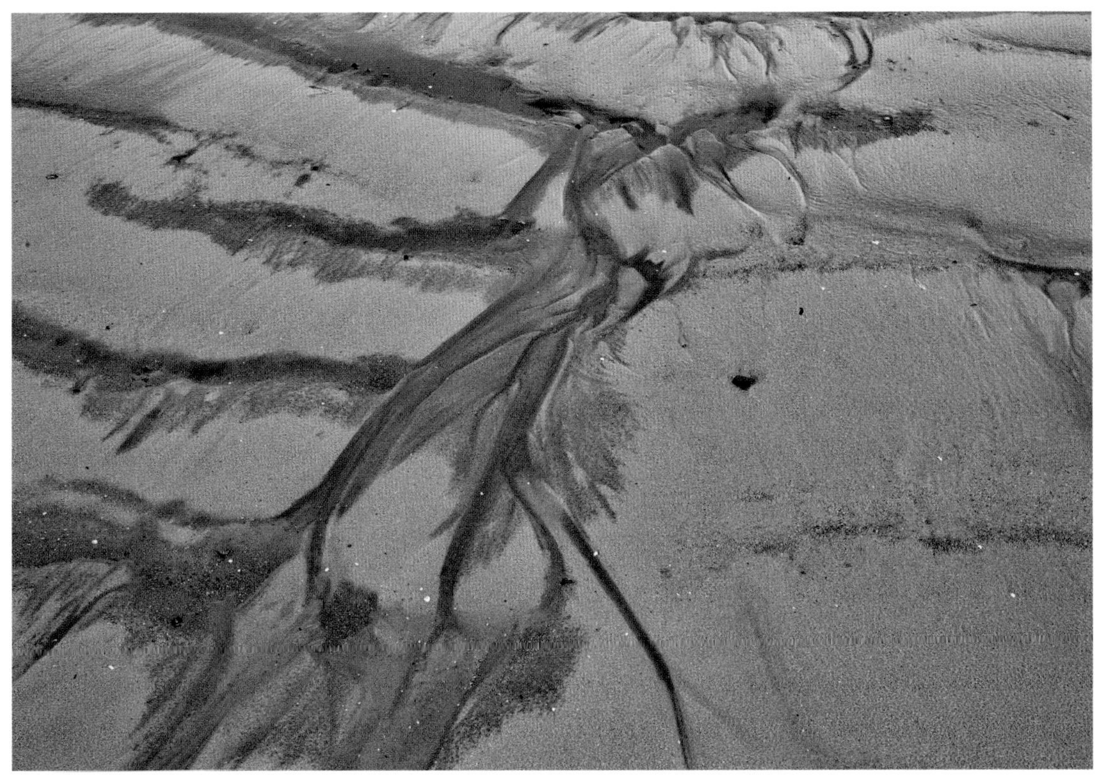

Plate 42 looks like an abstract painting. It's a result of water outflow at low tide exposing a heavy mineral—likely magnetite, a black-colored mineral commonly found on beaches. The outflow pattern looks like someone took a brush to a canvas because of all the swirls, fine lines, and changes in the tonal contrast.

PLATE | 42 |

Wind, a grass stem, and sand combine to create the sand sculpture seen in **Plate 43**. Circular, flat sand sculptures are common on the upper reaches of a beach, but undulating forms are not.

The relentless sea carved potholes up and down this Florida coastline composed of sandstone. Nature really put on a show (**Plate 44**) as a sculptor. The varied colors and sandstone formations were fantastic. One would guess it took tens of thousands of years, if not more, to achieve this seashore structure.

PLATE | 43 |

PLATE | 44 |

PLATE | 45 |

PLATE | 46 |

Plates 45 and **46** demonstrate the artistry of simple waves hitting the beach. The low-energy waves capture their surroundings via the colors reflected off their surfaces; their curvatures formed as a result of the shoreline's changing slope. Each image could be a painting expressing a calm, non-threatening sea.

Nature created a monochromatic, colored construct (light to dark brown) of the seashore as seen in **Plate 46**. The dark swash mark left by a previous tide offsets the light tan sand, producing a nice tonal contrast. I suspect an artist would go for the same tonal effect.

If I didn't know better, I would have thought this image (**Plate 47**) was a landform seen from several thousand feet up. In reality this beach scene is about 6 feet (1.8 m) long and 3 to 4 inches (8–10 cm) high. It's another example of nature, the sculptor, at work.

Sand channels parallel to the seashore are created by strong tidal currents. What you see is part of a channel with large ripple marks where water was carried into the channel, then out to sea.

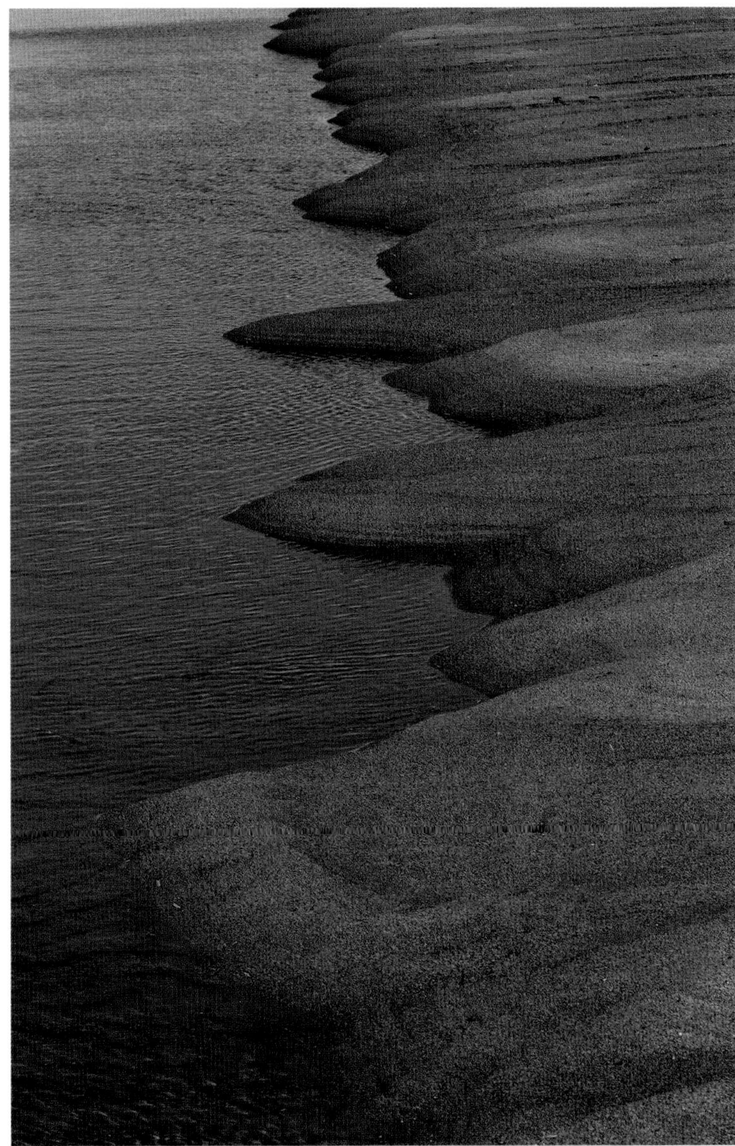

PLATE | 47 |

ROCKY SEASHORES & CLIFFS

It's always amazing to see thousands of rocks covering the shore from the tree line to the sea. Rocks come in all sorts of shapes: oval, spherical, flat, and blocky. Surf, waves, and/or river currents have acted as shaping agents via mechanical abrasion to round the ridges and corners of stones.

Rocky seashores are found mostly in the northern hemisphere above latitude 40 degrees. New England in the US, Southwestern England, Aryll in Scotland, and Omaha Beach in France are a few locations where rocky beaches are found. Beach rocks are mostly composed of granite, sandstone, basalt, shale, and quartz—those most resistant to erosion and weathering. Some rocks are composed of a pure mineral and others are mixed. The land profile of a rocky coast is a product of climate, wave patterns, and bedrock composition.

One of the most powerful experiences is to stand a few feet from the edge of a cliff hundreds of feet high, looking at the sea and crashing surf below and hearing the shrill cries of seagulls. Maybe this is why cliffs are such a big tourist draw. They combine beauty with a little danger.

Cliffs are found mainly in the middle latitudes where wave energy is high. These majestic landforms took millions of years, if not hundreds of millions of years, to form through abrasion and weathering on erodible, rocky headlands. High-energy waves battered the base of the headland, cutting a notch that grew slowly. Next, gravity took hold. The upper face sheared off to create a steep declivity landform, or cliff. Over time, the loose debris from the collapse was washed out to sea as the coast receded inland. Cliffs are also formed more violently. In England in the late Paleozoic era (~300 million years ago), boiling granite blew through the softer sedimentary surface rock to give rise to the granite cliffs of Cornwall in Southwestern England.

These cliffs range from around 200 feet (61 m) to the highest at 752 feet (224 m). We will explore some rocky coasts and cliffs in five areas of the US and abroad.

Maine Coast

When it comes to hard, rocky coastlines, Northern New England in the US is hard to beat. Even England, with 34 percent of its coastline categorized as rocky, can't compare to the 58 percent of hard rock along the Maine coast. Maine has about 2,000 miles of hard, rocky coast encompassing inlets, peninsulas, bays, and coves. **Plates 48** and **50** give glimpses of the rock shores in Acadia National Park, a popular tourist destination just east of Ellsworth, Maine. **Plate 50** shows the Bass Harbor Head Lighthouse. **Plate 48** is a view along Otter Point Trail. Bass Harbor Light was completed in 1876 and remains in operation today. Given the lighthouse's rather precipitous position, it's surprising that it's still standing.

Looking at a map of Maine, one is immediately struck by the numerous peninsulas from Freeport to Rockland, a distance of about fifty miles as the crow flies, or sixty-one miles via US Route 1. Of all the peninsulas, Damariscotta is one of the most scenic. At the very end of this twenty-three-mile-long peninsula is Pemaquid Point with its lighthouse. **Plate 49** depicts the view off the point enjoyed by two people who seem mesmerized by the angry sea. Here the rocky shore is composed of schist, striated rock formations (mainly metamorphic) that reach out into the sea. People of all ages love to climb these formations—especially photographers, I might add.

Turning out to sea, one finds Monhegan Island slightly less than twelve miles from Port Clyde and New Harbor, Maine. The island is a favorite of city dwellers and summer artists. Cliffs abound on its eastern shore: Whitehead, Blackhead, and Burnthead. **Plate 51** captures the eastern face of the island from a vantage point on Whitehead in early October.

Cape Ann, Massachusetts

Approximately 21,000 years ago the Laurentide Ice Sheet covered a great deal of North America: most of Canada, parts of the Midwest, the entire state of Maine, and stopped just south of Cape Cod in Massachusetts. It was part of the last glacial period called the Wisconsinan glacial stage (~120,000 to 11,700 years ago). Imagine a glacier near the seashore 1,500 feet (457 m) thick to around 13,000 feet (3.96 km) thick in some inland locations. At 13,000 feet, it's twice the height of Mt. Washington, the tallest mountain in the Eastern United States.

Have you ever walked a beach and come across humongous boulders weighing tons, just sitting there and not part of any headland? The answer to the mystery of their origin is found in glaciers. As glaciers move, they incorporate sediment at their base (cobbles, gravel, and small boulders). Further, they erode hillsides, where large boulders are picked up and settle on top of the glacier. Usually, small fragments are deposited a few miles from their source, but large fragments carried atop glaciers can be carried along for tens of miles, even hundreds. **Plates 52** and **53** capture such large boulders deposited on a beach on Cape Ann, a rocky landform an hour's drive north of Boston, while **Plates 54** and **55** show examples of small rocks deposited by glaciers eons ago.

Near and Far

The formations in **Plates 56–58** appear to be part of the same geographical landform; the rocks' color and fragmentation look very similar. Actually, **Plates 57** and **58** are the same landform, whereas **Plate 56** is about 3,100 miles (5,000 km) away. The bridge formation is north of Boston on the Nahant peninsula, while formations in **Plates 57** and **58** are in Tintagel, England, on the Cornish coast. Devonian rock and a granite backbone that intrudes into the surrounding sedimentary rock gave rise to these latter formations.

Bluffs & Cliffs

There is no clear-cut way to differentiate a cliff from a bluff. Here, cliff is defined as a bedrock landform with a steep vertical face, while a bluff is made from unconsolidated sediments (gravel, loose rock, clay, sand) with a gentle sloping face. When it comes to nature doing her handiwork, Cape Perpetua, two miles (3.2 km) south of Yachats, Oregon, along US Coastal Route 101, is in a class by itself. Its bluffs are simply stunning; see the hump-shaped bluff in **Plate 59**. It's not uncommon to see bluffs built on a rocky platform. **Plate 60** shows a bluff sitting on a bed of igneous rock with a ribbon of exposed sand on the bluffs just above the bedrock. In many places it's bedrock formation top to bottom, as seen along the Cabot Trail in Cape Breton Highlands National Park in Nova Scotia (**Plate 61**) and at Porthcurno in western Cornwall (**Plate 62**).

Coastal state highway US 1 in Northern California contains some big bluffs in Humboldt and Mendocino counties. The region is known as the Lost Coast because of depopulation in the 1930s. It is quite striking with bluffs running right down to the sea (**Plate 63**). This area is remote, with no roads in most of the coastal section.

Twenty species of birds love the Cliffs of Moher in Ireland; an estimated 30,000 birds call them home. **Plates 64** and **65** offer two different views of the cliffs. It's an amazing experience to look out to sea from these cliffs

PLATE | 48 |

PLATE | 49 |

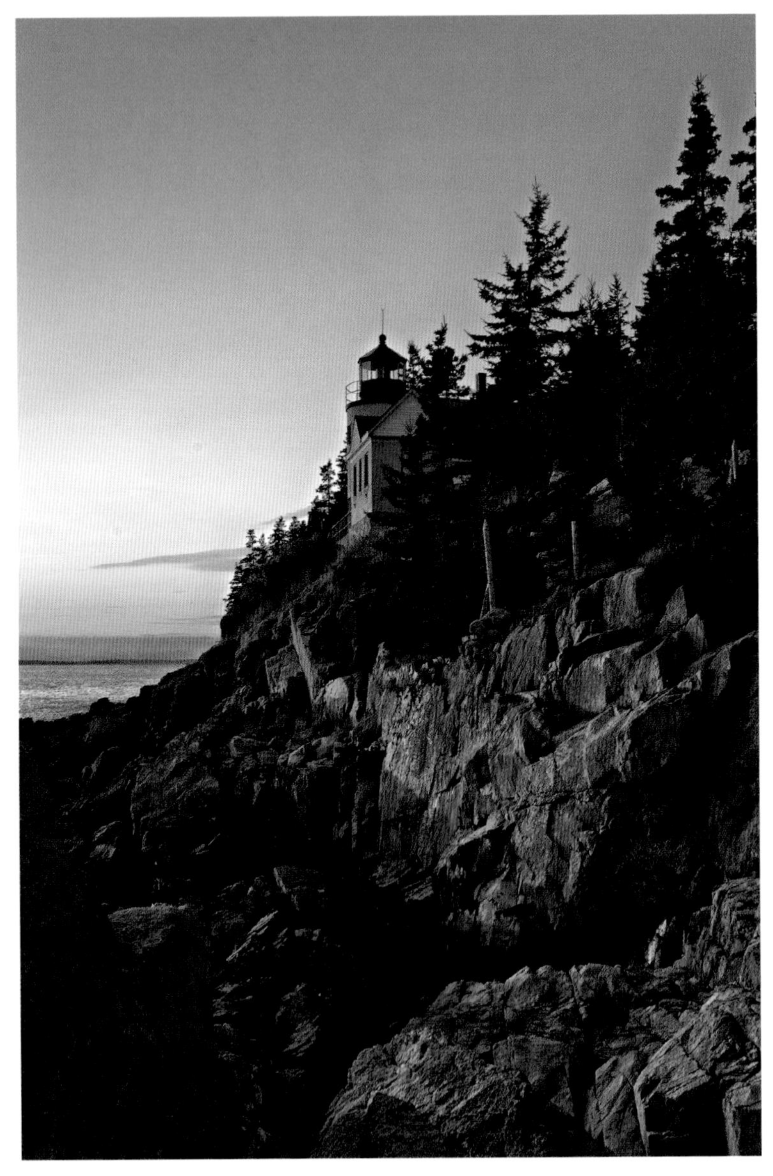

PLATE | 50 |

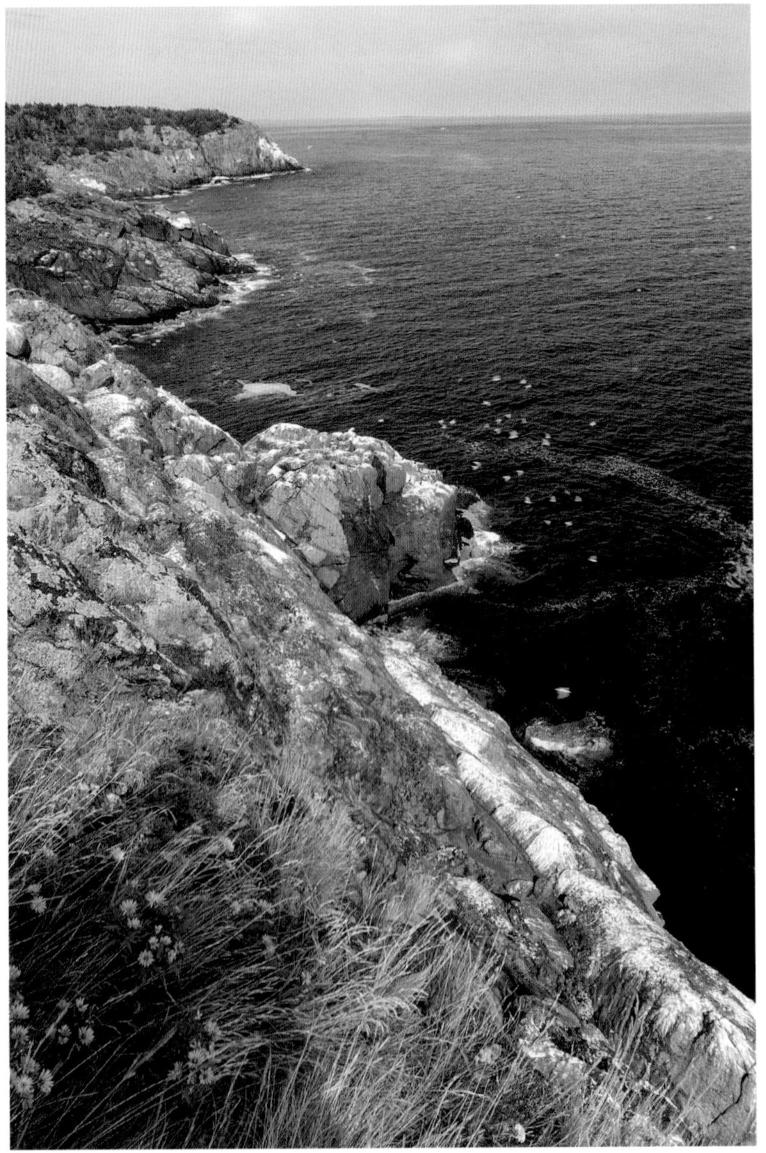

PLATE | 51 |

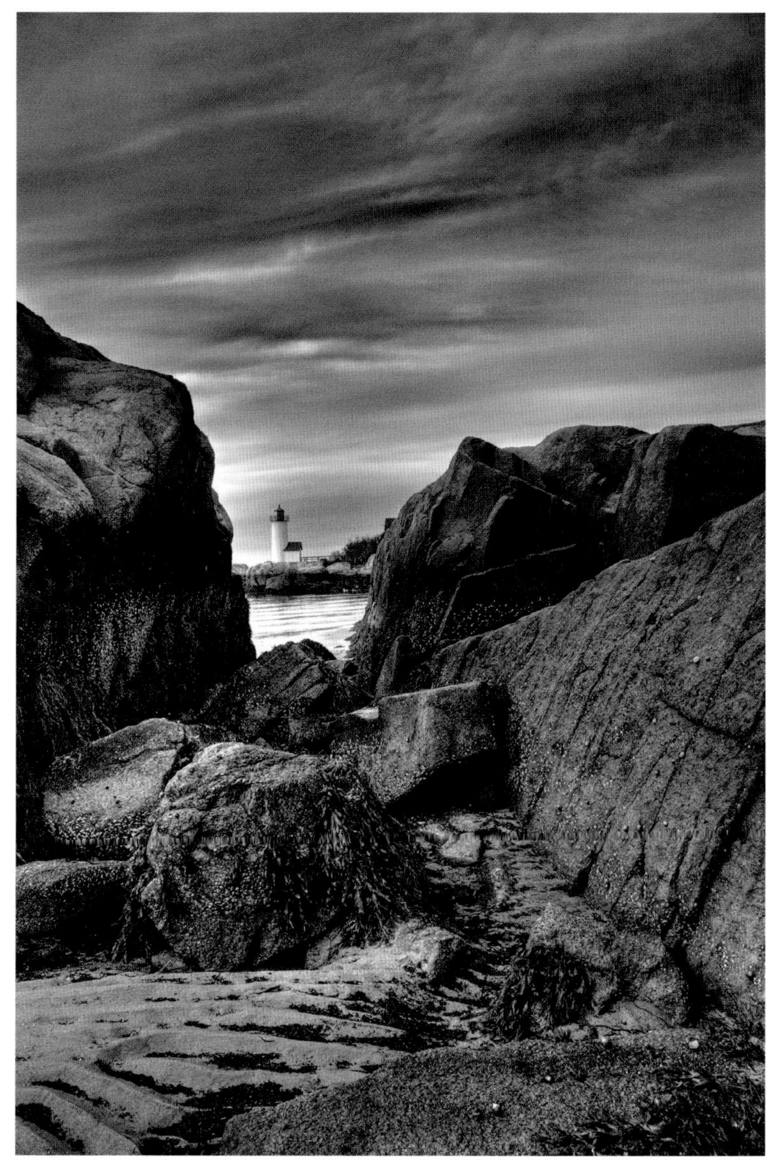

PLATE | 52 |

PLATE | 53 |

PLATE | 54 |

PLATE | 55 |

PLATE | 56 |

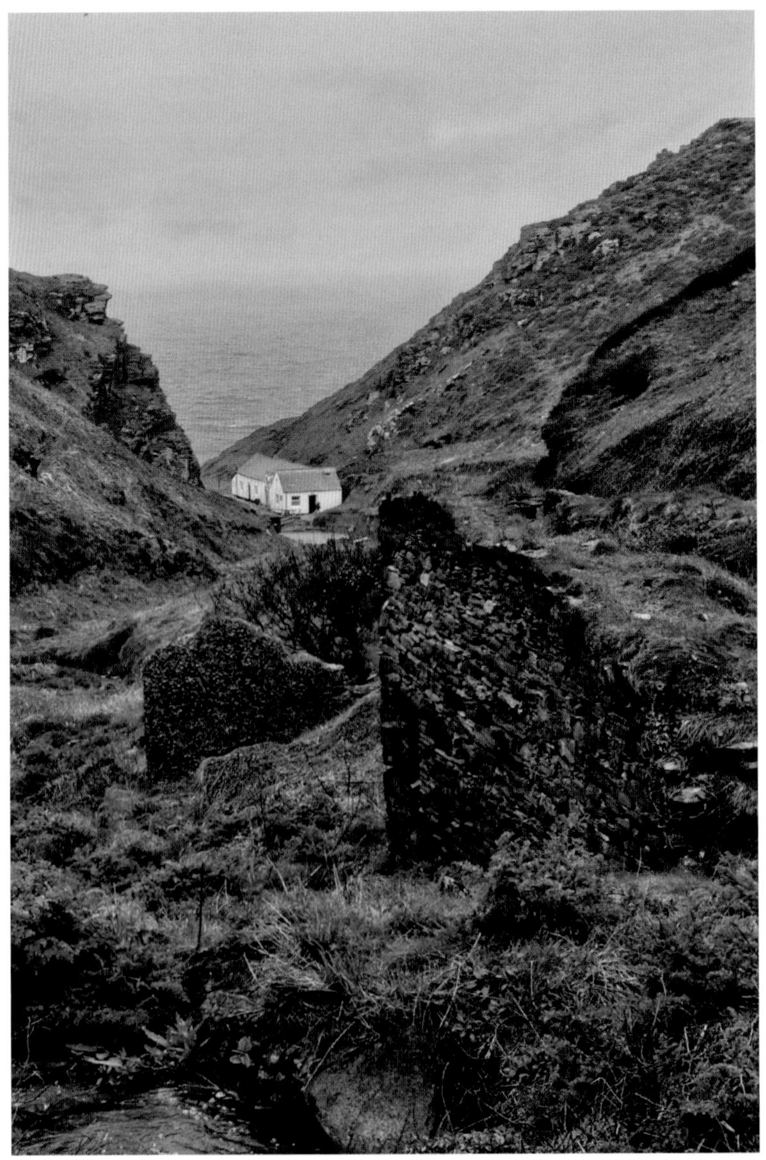

PLATE | 57 |

PLATE | 58 |

PLATE | 59 |

PLATE | 60 |

PLATE | 61 |

PLATE | 62 |

PLATE | 63 |

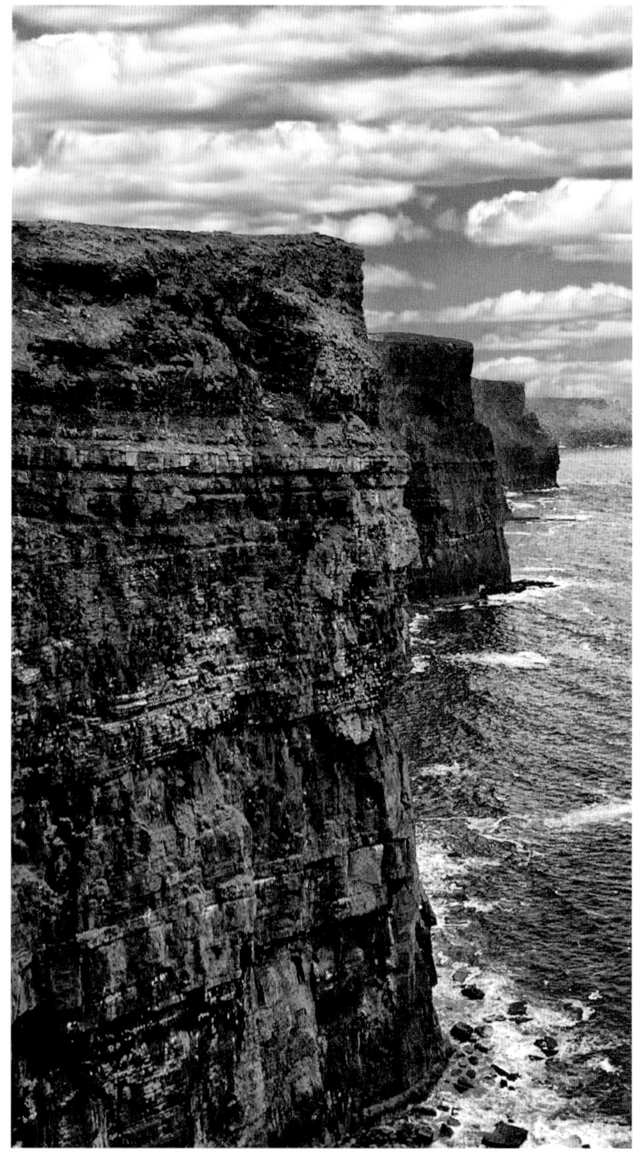

PLATE | 64 |

PLATE | 65 |

COASTAL INLETS

In these photos, we will explore some of the small harbors and coves of Maine, Massachusetts, and Nova Scotia, ending with the English coast.

Anyone who has visited Bar Harbor, Maine, wouldn't call the harbor small. In 2016 there were 117 scheduled cruise ship dockings. It's a picturesque harbor, as seen in the sunrise shot in **Plate 66**. Acadia National Park's many scenic trails lead to inlets. **Plate 67** shows an ocean inlet, near Schooner Head, which leads to a much larger inland pond.

New Harbor lies twenty miles south of Damariscotta on Route 130, a quintessential Maine lobstering village whose population hit 727 in 2014. The villagers' median age is sixty-nine years, but age doesn't seem to have slowed their pace; everyone seems busy. Except for a few new homes and maintenance work done on piers and dwellings, nothing of any major consequence seems to have brought change to New Harbor in the last thirty years, except perhaps a small convention hall built a few years ago.

Early morning is the best time to view the harbor. **Plate 68** was taken at 6:30 on a calm June morning where the only sounds were the cries of seagulls in search of food. The outer harbor is flanked with stony embankments that extend along the New Harbor shoreline. **Plates 69–70** are images of the same wharf in front of the Gosnold Arms Inn taken eight years apart, with the last taken in May 2016.

New Harbor's Back Cove is adjacent to the harbor on the right side looking seaward. As seen from **Plate 71**, the cove has a somewhat narrow opening to the sea, a rocky shoreline, and an oval-shaped embayment in which to anchor boats. It's an excellent place for small boats during storms. Back Cove is quintessential Maine, from the anchored boats, to the bridge spanning the rear of the cove, to an old barn sitting on the shoreline. It's also enjoyed by an occasional seagull (**Plate 72**).

The idyllic cove is home to a curiosity, namely a dilapidated row boat. I have been tracking this oddity for ten years now; wondering who owns it, who takes care of it, if anyone, and why it still exists. Every time I saw it, the boat was tied to a different wharf post, as if it had no home. **Plates 73-75** were taken in chronological order: June 2006, May 2012, and June 2016. In every picture, the floor of the boat appears either wet or damp, and it contains the same water scooper after ten years! Isn't that strange?

Plate 76 was taken looking through the Thompson Boat House at a small trawler anchored in the cove. The boat house has been an unchanged fixture here for at least thirty years. In that time span, I don't recall it ever being locked.

PLATE | 66 |

PLATE | 67 |

PLATE | 68 |

PLATE | 69 |

PLATE | 70 |

PLATE | 71 |

PLATE | 72 |

PLATE | 73 |

PLATE | 74 |

PLATE | 75 |

PLATE | 76 |

If you like harbor views, you'll like Mackerel Cove, which lies about twenty-one miles (thirty-four km) down Route 24 from Brunswick, Maine. The drive to the cove is scenic, passing through Orr's Island, then over a bridge onto Bailey Island until you reach Mackerel Cove (**Plates 77** and **78**). Route 24 sits high up and looks down at the cove, which is packed with lobster boats during lobstering season from the first week of May to the first week of December. Although lobstering is permitted year-round, May to December is the best time to lobster.

Nothing characterizes the Massachusetts coastline better than its marshy inlets from Plum Island on the north shore down to Plymouth and Cape Cod on the south shore. Winding inlets can run inland from one hundred feet to several miles. The longest inlets are usually small rivers draining into the sea, and their banks are surrounded by wide fields of marsh cordgrass and home to birdlife. **Plates 79** and **80** depict an inlet in East Chatham, Massachusetts, taken at slightly different angles and focal lengths. **Plate 79** was taken in late December when the beach grass had turned a rust-colored brown, while the infrared image (**Plate 80**) was taken late in the day at the end of October, hence its shadowed foreground.

One would be remiss not to include Rockport Harbor among the coastal indentations. It is quite picturesque, and Motif #1, the red shed in **Plate 81**, is probably one of the world's most painted and photographed buildings. **Plate 81** is an HDR image enhanced to produce a somewhat dramatic look with a threatening sky and a defiant-looking shed.

Three thousand miles or so across the Atlantic, one sees coastal indentations on the Devon and Cornish coasts that are somewhat different than those of Maine and Massachusetts. Beach geology and landforms differ widely. **Plates 82** and **83** show the high chalk cliffs that border the shallow harbor in Beer, England, on the Devon coast. Note the lack of wharfs; the boats just sit on the beach and wait for the tide to come in. Many small fishing villages on the southern coast have breakwaters (rock barriers) to protect the harbor or cove, but no wharfs per se.

If you watch *Doc Martin* on British or American public television, the imaginary village of Portwenn is, in reality, Port Isaac, located on the southwestern section of the Cornish coast. **Plate 84** is a street view adjacent to the harbor. **Plate 85** shows the hillside part of Port Isaac where some scenes were filmed. While Massachusetts has marshy inlets, the UK's Devon and Cornish coasts have rocky coves. **Plates 86** and **87** are examples of such coves. It's usually a steep climb down to the shore, so most accessible coves have staircases. Brits love their ocean walkways, which go for miles. People visit these rocky coves for the express purpose of finding seashells and other flotsam or simply to take a walk and enjoy the breathtaking views.

Anyone traveling to Nova Scotia has undoubtedly heard of Peggy's Cove. It's a main attraction lying twenty-six miles (42 km) southwest of downtown Halifax. From its beginning, its economy has revolved around fishing, mainly lobstering. After WWII it slowly became dependent on tourism and remains so, even though lobstering is still done. The fishing industry, however small, has helped it retain most of its picturesque charm. Plus, strict land-use regulations prevent developers from disfiguring the village with commercial enterprises. **Plates 88** and **89** attest to the picturesque charm of Peggy's Cove. The boats, buildings, and homes all contribute to the peaceful scene, and the clouds and fog add a little mystery.

PLATE | 77 |

PLATE |78|

PLATE | 79 |

PLATE |80|

PLATE | 81 |

PLATE |82|

PLATE | 83 |

PLATE | 84 |

PLATE |85 |

PLATE | 86 |

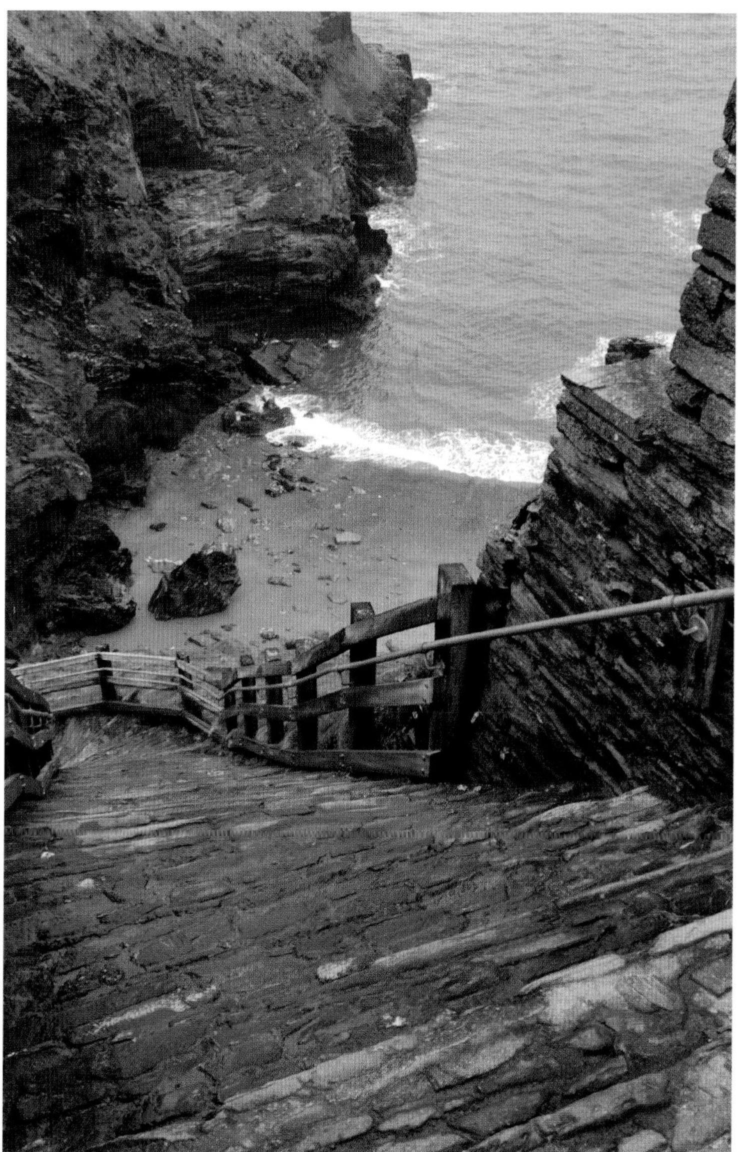

PLATE | 87 |

PLATE | 88 |

PLATE | 89 |

LIGHTHOUSES

Lighthouses are like sentinels; they act as navigational aids to passing ships and pleasure boats. There are electronic navigational aids such as GPS and VHF radio; however, computer breakdown, interference from solar activity, and severe storms can lead to loss of communication. It's reassuring to have physical aids such as lighthouses and buoys to guide mariners and fishermen.

Up and down the Atlantic seaboard are hundreds of lights (lighthouse keepers referred to lighthouses as lights). New England alone has 216 or so lights with approximately 160 still active. Maine and Massachusetts have the largest number of active lights, approximately sixty-four and forty-seven, respectively. It's hard to come up with a precise count because they are owned by the government, private residents, and nonprofit groups.

Annisquam Lighthouse

Formerly known as Wigwam Point, Annisquam Harbor Light Station in Gloucester, Massachusetts, was established in 1801 with a $2,000 congressional appropriation. It was rebuilt in 1851, again as a wooden structure, and in 1897 a brick structure was built on the same foundation as the two previous structures. Over the next hundred years an automated fog horn was installed, a fifth-order Fresnel lens was installed in 1856, and the light was automated in 1974. In 1987 the light was added to the National Registry of Historic Places. In 2000, 3,000 bricks were replaced as part of the 41-foot (13 m) tower's complete restoration. **Plates 90–92** show different views of this picturesque lighthouse.

Pemaquid Lighthouse

At the tip of Pemaquid Point, near the very end of the Damariscotta peninsula in Bristol, Maine, one comes to the Pemaquid Light, one of the most photographed lighthouses in Maine, if not the US. The light was first built around 1827, then rebuilt in 1835 because salt water used in the mortar caused deterioration. Today's light is still the 38-foot (12 m) tower equipped with the Fresnel lens installed in 1856 and automated in 1934. The tower's interior brick veneer and cast-iron staircase, added during the late nineteenth century, were fully restored in 2010.

The light sits on rock sediment from the Silurian period (430 million year ago), which went through a metamorphic process about 360 million years ago. Molten rock mixed with molten igneous rock formed twisted and folded, striated bands consisting mainly of feldspar, quartz, and mica. These formations led from the lighthouse to the sea to make a dramatic foreground for the lighthouse. **Plates 93–95** are different views of Pemaquid light. **Plate 93** was shot early in the morning at the base of the rocky outcropping leading away from the light. Minimalism defines **Plate 94** with just a simple cross-section of the rock tower against a pastel-colored sky. **Plate 95** was shot at night using a ten-second exposure and light painting on the frontal portion of the lighthouse..

Ponce de Leon Inlet Light

In Ponce Inlet, Florida, stands the Ponce de Leon Inlet Light, the second tallest lighthouse in the United States at 175 feet (53 m), second to Cape Hatteras Light in North Carolina at 207 feet (63 m). The current structure was completed in 1887 and its kerosene lamp could be seen twenty miles (thirty-two km) out to sea. It wasn't until 1933 that a third-order Fresnel lens was installed with a 500-watt lamp. In 1970 the Coast Guard abandoned the light but restored it to service in 1982. Ponce de Leon Light was placed on the National Registry of Historic Places in 1972, one of eleven lighthouses so designated. **Plates 96–97** show exterior and interior views. The view of the 203 stairs is quite dramatic looking down from the top.

Stage Harbor Light

In 1878, Congress approved $10,000 to construct a light at Stage Harbor in Chatham, Massachusetts. It went into service in July 1880 at a cost of $9,862.74. The light has a fifth-order Fresnel lens that was visible for twelve nautical miles (fourteen miles or twenty-three km). The light was of modest size and stayed in service until 1933. It is now a private residence. **Plate 98** of the Stage Harbor Light was taken at sunrise.

PLATE | 90 |

PLATE | 91 |

PLATE | 92 |

PLATE | 93 |

PLATE | 94 |

PLATE | 95 |

PLATE | 96 |

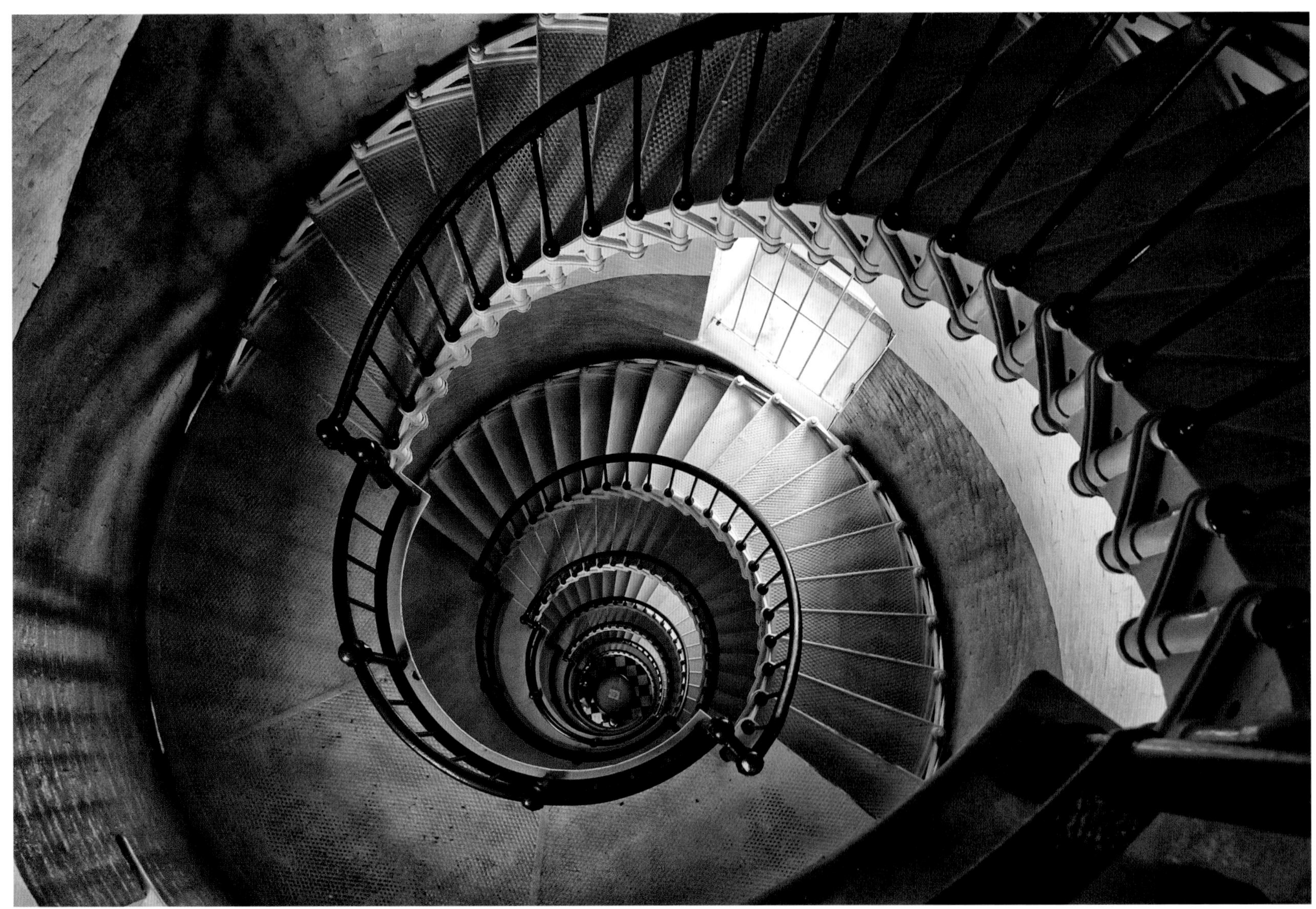

PLATE | 97 |

PLATE | 98 |

Peggy's Point Lighthouse

Just up from Peggy's Cove in Nova Scotia is the Peggy's Point Light (**Plate 99**). The octagonal tower rises to a modest 49 feet (15 m) and is painted in classic red and white. The current light was built in 1914–15 out of reinforced concrete. It has since provided a beacon to ships entering St. Margaret's Bay. The light was fully automated in 1958. Daily visitors pour over the rocky outcrop to photograph the light in the summer months. It is probably one of the most photographed structures in Atlantic Canada.

Monhegan Island Light

The current circular structure of the Monhegan Light on Monhegan Island, Maine, (**Plate 100**) was built in 1850 out of granite blocks; the island is one big, granite bedrock. At 47 feet (14 m) tall, it is the second tallest lighthouse in Maine. Sitting at the highest point on the island, the view of the island and Manana Island across the harbor is breathtaking on a clear day. The climb to the light is well worth the effort.

Portland Head Lighthouse

Visitors to Portland Head Light on Cape Elizabeth, Maine, number more than one million per year. It sits on a headland at the entrance to Portland Harbor, which is part of Casco Bay. In 1787, George Washington established a $1,500 fund to build the light. It was completed in January 1791, making it Maine's oldest light. The tower is now as it was in 1791 except for the upgraded beacon system, last done in 1991. This majestic set of buildings is perched on a cliff (**Plate 101**). Shining out to the sea, its beacon can be seen for twenty-four nautical miles (twenty-eight miles, forty-four km) by ships in Casco Bay. The tower is joined by a museum and maintenance barn (**Plate 102**).

Cape Blanco Lighthouse

Completed in December 1870, Cape Blanco Light (**Plate 103**) stands on the farthest point west on the Oregon coast, one-and-a-half miles into the Pacific Ocean from Oregon's southern coast. The light sits on a 200-foot-high, chalky white cliff. Both the foundation and the 59-foot (18-m) tower were constructed out of 200,000 bricks made nearby at a cost of $25 per thousand delivered—even at fifty times the price, it would be good deal today. The station was automated and de-staffed in 1980 and placed on the National Register of Historic Places in April 1993. It is still a functioning lighthouse.

Yaquina Head Light

This light is located near the mouth of the Yaquina River near Newport, Oregon. At a height of 93 feet (28 m) the Yaquina Light (**Plate 104**) is the tallest in Oregon. It was completed in August 1873 employing a fixed, first-order Fresnel lens made in Paris in 1868. The light is active two seconds on, two seconds off, two seconds on, then fourteen seconds off. It's still in use today, visible nineteen miles (thirty-one km) out to sea. In 1993 Yaquina Light was placed on the National Register of Historic Places.

PLATE |99|

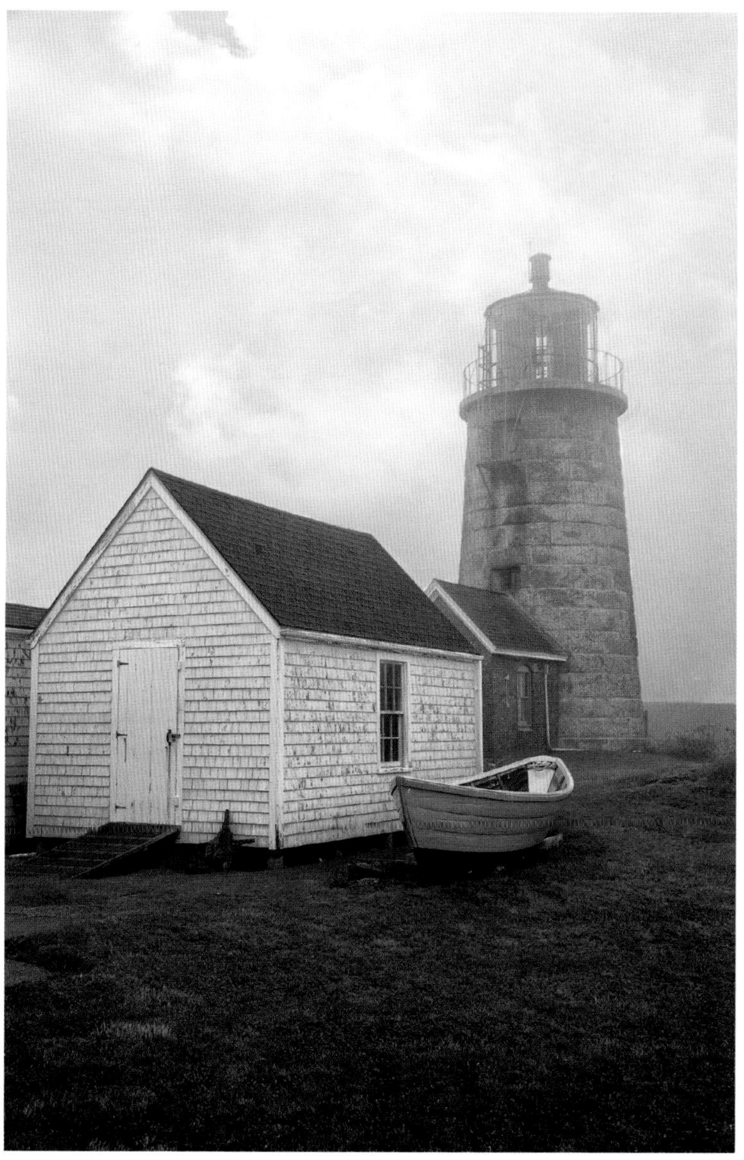

PLATE |100|

PLATE | 101 |

PLATE | 102 |

PLATE | 103 |

PLATE | 104 |

St. Augustine Light

One can't miss the St. Augustine Light at the north end of Anastasia Island in St. Augustine, Florida. Its 165-foot (50-m) structure looks like a black-and-white barber's pole topped with a red cap (**Plate 105**). The tower was built using brick from Alabama, granite from Georgia, 214 spiral cast-iron steps forged in Philadelphia, and a first-order Fresnel lens produced in France. Sixty-two years would pass before the light was electrified in 1936, and then another twenty years before the light was automated. The US Coast Guard declared it surplus, and St. Johns County bought the light in 1970. A massive restoration effort by St. Augustine's Junior Service League restored the tower and its surrounding property. It has been on the National Register of Historic Places since 1981.

Tybee Island Lighthouse

Tybee Light is on the northeast end of Tybee Island, Georgia, next to the Savannah River. The current structure (**Plate 106**) has the black-white-black daymark banding first used in 1916. The brick tower is 154 feet (47 m); it contains 178 stairs and a first-order Fresnel lens whose beam can be seen up to eighteen miles (twenty-nine km) out to sea. The current light is the fourth one at this station; the first was built in 1736. Electrification in 1933 ended the need for the three keepers. The station, maintained by the Tybee Island Historical Society, is open to the public. It remains an active lighthouse and navigational aid. The entrance is through a small room attached to its base. **Plate 107** has a Hopperesque feel given its colors and the buildings' architectural simplicity. Edward Hopper was a noted American painter.

Heceta Head Light

Heceta Head Light is nestled midway up a 205-foot (62-m)-tall headland on the Oregon coast. Seen from a distance, the lighthouse scene is absolutely beautiful with its white buildings and red roofs set against a greenish-brown background of rocks, vegetation, and trees (**Plate 108**). With a crew of fifty-six men, construction started in 1892 on the light and lightkeeper cottages. Materials were brought in by boat, weather permitting, or by a coastal route from Florence, thirteen miles south of Heceta Head. Stones came from a nearby river and bricks came from San Francisco. By August 1893, at a cost of $80,000, the lighthouse and six additional buildings were completed. The 56-foot (17-m)-tall lighthouse has a beam visible twenty-four miles (thirty-nine km) out to sea, making it the strongest light on the Oregon coast. For roughly two years, starting in 2011, the light was closed for a major restoration. Today the state of Oregon maintains the light.

Nubble Light (Cape Neddick Light)

Nubble Light is an iconic American lighthouse on Nubble Island, a stone's throw from York, Maine (**Plate 109**). A major tourist attraction, an estimated half-million people visit every year.

On a steep rocky islet, the tower sits 88 feet (27 m) above sea level. It still employs a fourth-order Fresnel lens, the same as the original that was damaged and replaced in 1928. The light flashes three seconds on and three seconds off. The small, bright red oil house was added in 1902 and a boathouse and boat-slip in 1888. A kerosene vapor lamp was used until the station was electrified in 1938. In 1998 the townspeople adopted the station under the Maine Lights Program. Still an active lighthouse, it was placed on the National Register of Historic Places in 1985.

PLATE | 105 |

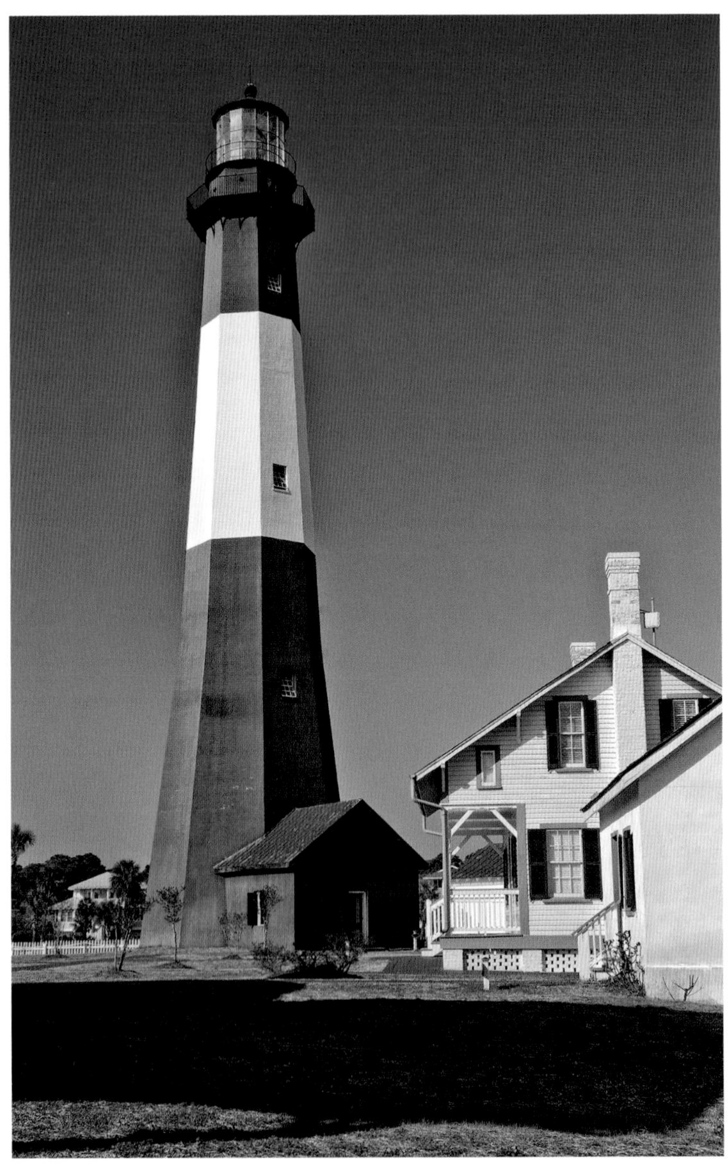

PLATE | 106 |

PLATE | 107 |

PLATE |108|

PLATE | 109 |

SEASHORE FINDS

One of the more rewarding experiences for a traveler is to discover something unusual that is not designated an "attraction." It could be a landscape scene, an object, or some physical structure. Discovering "finds" is part of the fun of traveling back roads along the sea coast with camera in hand.

Plate 110 depicts a seaside chapel at the end of walled-in field adjacent to a deserted road outside Ponce, Puerto Rico. **Plate 111** is a set of cabanas in the small English village of Branscombe on the Devon coast—both are unexpected scenes. Piers come in all sizes (see **Plates 112-115**). What's different here is that they were not visible from a main road. The scene in **Plate 116** is somewhat surrealistic in that the two highways, leading to Key West, Florida, seem to go on forever, and a person was walking on the road on the right. Where are the cars? To photograph this scene, I had to travel a back road, then climb up a flight of stairs to the roadway on the right. It looked like something out of Rod Serling's *The Twilight Zone*, a television series in the early 1960s.

Monhegan Island, off the Maine coast, has less than a half-dozen or so dirt roads that make for interesting tours of the island. In spite of its small size (0.5 square miles, or 1.3 square km) the island has many interesting scenes to discover, both man-made and natural. **Plates 117** and **118** were taken on the island. Both images remind one of an Edward Hopper painting. It wasn't until several years later that I discovered that the cottage in **Plate 118** is called Uncle Henry's Cottage; it has an iconic presence. When passing by ocean inlets on back roads, keep an eye out for wooden piers or walkways used to access small boats docked in these inlets. In good light, a walkway surrounded by marsh grass can create a scene with a pastoral feel as seen in **Plate 120**. It's the soft light during the latter part of day that's essential here.

Outside of New Bedford, Massachusetts, are the remains of Fort Phoenix in Fairhaven, where the first navel battle of the American Revolution occurred. The fort was destroyed on September 5–6, 1778, but later rebuilt and named Fort Phoenix after the mythical bird. **Plate 121** is an infrared image of the fort grounds that feels rugged and romantic, due, in part, to the wind-blown tree and the tonal content.

Out of nowhere, traveling along the Bay of Fundy in New Brunswick, sat this rather large tug boat **(Plate 122)** about a quarter-mile from the shoreline. The boat's placement was promotional, since a maritime ship museum was nearby.

While three pelicans enjoy the good life sitting quite comfortably on three lamp lights (**Plate 123)**, I couldn't help comparing them to the three clammers (**Plate 124**) doing back-breaking digging for clams on the flats in Gloucester, Massachusetts. Nature takes a rest while men work to pay the bills.

Outside the village of Dinard in Normandy, France, an old, deserted tidal warehouse was surrounded on one side by a fog bank and on the other by marshland with the moon sitting on high (**Plate 125)**. It was a poetic scene that begged to be photographed. While traveling up Route 337 in Nova Scotia, out of the corner of my eye, I caught a vacant, somewhat collapsed fishing shack and pier sticking out from the shore. I felt the scene (**Plate 126)** was made for an infrared image.

Moving from the shore, a little house was visible on top of Manana Island in Maine (**Plate 127)**. The lonely shack, an empty landscape, and ominous clouds instill a sense of isolation. Manana Island is next door to Monhegan Island, Maine.

Can you guess why **Plate 128** looks strange? It's the position of the old Adirondack chairs. They are positioned for people to look inland, not seaward. Who goes to the beach to look inland?

PLATE | 110 |

PLATE | 111 |

PLATE | 112 |

PLATE | 113 |

PLATE | 114 |

NO PEDESTRIANS
WITHIN 20 FT. OF PIER
FALLING OBJECTS
MAY BE HAZARDOUS
DANGER!
FALLING DEBRIS HAZARD
NO LOITERING
UNDER PIER

PLATE | 115 |

PLATE | 116 |

PLATE | 117 |

PLATE | 118 |

The 200-year-old home pictured in **Plate 119** was found in Clovelly on the Devon coast, an English village dating to the thirteenth century. It has steep, narrow streets and no motorized vehicles except one to bring tourists up from the village. Donkeys pulling sledges piled with supplies service the village's fifty-odd homes.

Although Clovelly is listed in many tour books as a place to see, it's impossible for any tour book to do it justice. Throughout the village are many incredible scenes of daily life—a photographer's delight.

PLATE | 119 |

PLATE |120|

PLATE | 121 |

PLATE | 122 |

PLATE | 123 |

PLATE | 124 |

PLATE | 125 |

PLATE | 126 |

PLATE | 127 |

PLATE | 128 |

FOGGY DAYS

There is something mysterious about a fog-shrouded harbor or shoreline. We can see only pieces of things, hence the question of what else is there, real or imaginary. Thick fog can disrupt our orientation, especially if there are no objects around to guide us. Yet fog also has a calming affect; everything seems quieter and at rest.

Fog can be hazy (light fog) with moderate visibility or dense with poor visibility—what you see is a blank, grayish-white wall. The following photos explore all these fog conditions.

Near the Shore

Plate 129 shows Dartmouth Castle in Dartmouth, England. The background is engulfed in haze while closer to the viewer the fog is barely noticeable. A similar situation exists in the harbor scene of a small village on the Devon coast (**Plate 130**). The foreground is reasonably clear while the background is quite foggy. As you look farther away, you see through many more layers of haze; the fog becomes more pronounced.

Plates 131-132 go from a light haze encompassing a seascape with glacial boulders in the foreground to a thick fog hovering just off a rocky shore battered by waves. **Plate 132** evokes a strong sense of drama and danger; the sea seems able to swallow you up if you ventured too far onto the rocks. **Plate 131**, on the other hand, gives one a sense of peace and a hint of the unknown

Boats

Plates 133–137 are primarily about boats surrounded by light to moderate to heavy fog. The row boat and sloop (**Plates 133 and 134**) stand out in these images since the background is softened by the haze.

The *Friendship of Salem*, 171 feet (52 m) long, is docked at the Salem Maritime National Historic Site established in 1938 in Salem, Massachusetts (**Plate 135**). The background is a wall of fog, causing the ship and warehouse to stand out. The fog strengthens the image by separating the ship and warehouse from distracting, background elements.

Plates 136-137 are infrared images of boats moored in several small harbors along the Nova Scotia coast. They evoke a feeling of isolation and emptiness.

PLATE | 129 |

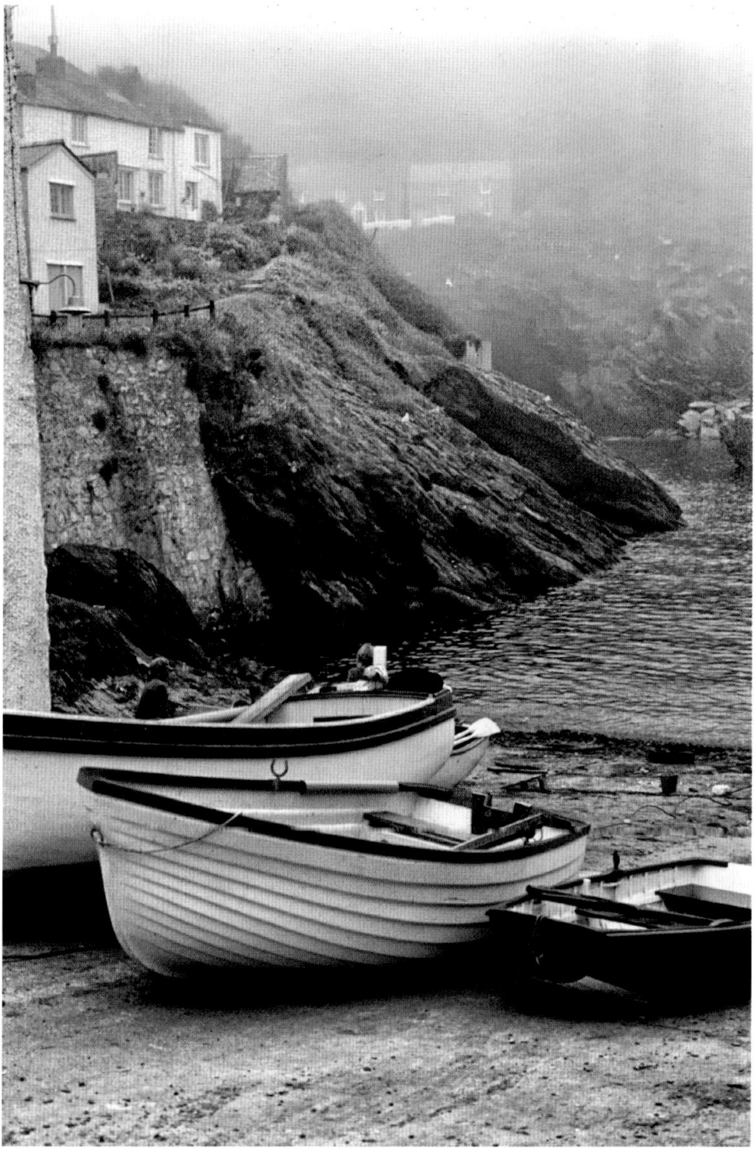

PLATE | 130 |

PLATE | 131 |

PLATE | 132 |

PLATE | 133 |

PLATE | 134 |

PLATE | 135 |

PLATE | 136 |

PLATE | 137 |

Harbors

Photographs of harbors inundated by fog can look like paintings due to the reduced sharpness and contrast. Thick, early morning fog often lasts until midmorning before it burns off, so there is time to capture foggy scenes in the morning without getting up at dawn. Late in the day, a cold front can move in and cause foggy conditions as well. **Plates 138–141** depict harbors along the Maine and Nova Scotia coasts.

Look carefully at **Plate 137** and then look at **Plate 138**. The two boats in the foreground are the same in both images, yet they look different because of the perspective and use of infrared versus color imaging.

Plate 139 was taken at Pemaquid Harbor on the Damariscotta peninsula in Maine under a heavy fog, which turned the scene into a minimalistic image with only a few well-placed objects.

Late evening fog on Monhegan Island (**Plate 140**) resulted in an image of the harbor that looked like a painting by James Whistler from his famous Nocturne series. The lights from the boats, the fog, calm waters, and foreground beach came together in a painterly scene. It is a scene that undoubtedly can never be precisely duplicated.

Early evening fog engulfed the harbor at New Harbor, Maine as the tide rolled in. The soft focus of **Plate 141** created a dreamy look. In addition, the boats appear surrealistic, coming out of nowhere.

At the Beach

Hardly anyone goes to the beach on a foggy day, but those who do may find some interesting images. When I first saw **Plate 142** I immediately asked myself, are these three people together? I concluded they must be. The image has the soft quality of a painting.

Plate 143 looks like an impressionistic painting of a family having fun at the beach. One is drawn immediately to the people since the heavy fog blocks out any distractions coming from the background. In addition, the people are positioned against a light background, creating a contrast that emphasizes the figures. The image was taken at Good Harbor Beach in Gloucester, Massachusetts.

PLATE | 138 |

PLATE | 139 |

PLATE | 140 |

PLATE | 141 |

PLATE | 142 |

PLATE | 143 |

SUNRISE, SUNSET & MOON OVER THE BAY

Red sky in the morning, sailors take warning,
Red sky at night, a sailor's delight.

Sunrise

City dwellers and suburbanites rarely get to see the fiery display of a rising sun, best seen over a body of water. At first a reddish-orange or reddish-pink band of color spreads across the horizon (**Plate 144**). Ten to fifteen minutes before sunrise, the diffracted light has a reddish-yellow tint with the stars still visible in the background; it's quite wonderful to experience.

Plates 145–146 were taken just as the solar disk came over the horizon. **Plate 145** was taken at 1/125 sec, at f/14, and a focal length of 170 mm, while **Plate 146** was taken at 1/30 second at f/14, and at a focal length of 200 mm. Image **145** was over Cape Cod Bay and **146** was taken at Good Harbor Beach in Gloucester, Massachusetts, with the Thatcher Island twin lights in the background.

Storm clouds coming in from the west lit up the sky (**Plate 147)** as the sunlight was reflected off them in this early morning shot; the whole sky was red, a warning to sailors and lobstermen of a possible impending storm.

Sunset

Sunsets can be spectacular, but it all depends on the weather and cloud situation. **Plate 148** caught the sinking sun at Heceta Head off the Oregon coast with camera settings at 1/125 second, at f/11, and a focal length of 28 mm.

Moon over the Bay

A full moon casting its light across Cape Cod Bay creates an unforgettable scene, especially when the moonlight is complimented by a dimly lit shoreline (**Plate 149**). It's the kind of scene I think artists Joseph Turner or Jean Millet would paint; things are revealed, yet things remain hidden. An aperture of f/14, an exposure of 20 seconds, and a focal length of 35 mm were the key camera settings.

A supermoon occurs when the moon is full and makes its closest approach to Earth, 220,000 miles (357,000 km), in its elliptical orbit around the Earth. Supermoons occur every fourteen full moons. **Plate 150** captures the supermoon just as it popped above the horizon looking across Cape Cod Bay. Its odd appearance is due to partial masking by a cloud in this ½-second exposure at an f/11 aperture. Just seventeen minutes later, the supermoon was well above the horizon, (**Plate 151**). The latter looks like a painting with the moon just hanging above the sea. But something is wrong with image; there is no moonlight reflecting off the ocean. It's a montage of two images. The supermoon image was captured using a 400 mm focal length, which completely isolated it from the sea. Then an image of the sea was taken; next the two were superimposed to create **Plate 151**.

PLATE | 144 |

PLATE | 145 |

PLATE | 146 |

PLATE | 147|

PLATE | 148 |

PLATE | 149 |

PLATE | 150 |

PLATE | 151 |

APPENDIX

Types of Rocks

Igneous rock is formed through the process of cooling and solidification of magma or lava from volcanic activity. Rocks can form with or without crystallization, either below the surface as intrusive, or on the Earth's surface as extrusive formations.

Metamorphic rock is formed via physical/chemical changes of existing rocks (sedimentary, igneous, and metamorphic) where rocks are subjected to heat greater than 150–200°C and pressure near or above 1.5 million psi (pounds per square inch). This transforms existing rocks in a process called metamorphism, which literally means a change in form. Such transformations occur deep within the Earth's crust and involve tectonic plate movements.

Sedimentary rock is formed through a process of deposition (coming together) of materials followed by cementation of the material to form rocks either at the Earth's surface or within bodies of water. Sedimentation contains many different processes that cause both minerals and organic materials to settle (collect) in one place as sediment. The collection process can be driven by such agents as water, ice, and glaciers. Sedimentation may also occur as minerals precipitate from water or the shells of aquatic creatures settle out of suspension. About eight percent of Earth's crust is sedimentary rock, with the bulk being igneous and metamorphic rock.

Kinds of Seashore Sands and Rocks by Size

Sand: very coarse sand 0.04–0.08" (1–2 mm), coarse sand 0.02–04" (0.5–1 mm), medium sand 0.01–0.02" (0.25–0.5 mm); fine sand 0.005–0.01" (0.125–0.25 mm), very fine sand 0.002–0.005" (0.0625–0.125 mm)

Boulders: greater than 10" (>256 mm)
Cobbles: 2.5–10" (64–256 mm)
Pebbles: 0.16–2.5" (4–64 mm)
Granules: 0.08–016" (2–4 mm)

Types of Minerals

Feldspars are aluminum silicate minerals that come in several compositions, $CaAI_2Si_2O_8$, $KAISi_3O_8$, and $NaAISi_3O_8$. The light tan Al-silicates make up around 60 percent of the Earth's crust and are found everywhere, usually as veins in magma and igneous rocks in both intrusive and extrusive formations.

Garnet is a group of silicate minerals which, because of their hardness, have been used both as abrasives and as gemstones. Their variety of colors includes red, orange, yellow, green, purple, brown, blue, black, pink, and colorless, with reddish colors the most common. Garnets are a family of neosilicates with the general formula $X_3Y_2(SiO_4)_3$. The X sites are usually occupied by

Ca, Mg, Fe, or Mn cations while the Y sites are occupied by Al, Fe, or Cr cations. Differences in cations and crystal structures account for the variety of colors of garnets.

Ilmenite is composed of titanium-iron with a general formula $FeTiO_3$. It is slightly magnetic and gray or black in color.

Magnetite is one of the main iron ores whose chemical formula is Fe_3O_4. It is brown or black-brown in color. Small grains of the mineral magnetite appear in almost all igneous and metamorphic rocks.

Quartz is the second most abundant mineral in the Earth's continental crust after feldspar. It exists in crystal structures composed of repeat units of SiO_4.

High Dynamic Range (HDR)

HDR is a method used to extend the luminosity range captured in a digital image. Normally three to seven images are taken of the same scene using one f-stop or less between images. Special software is used to combine these HDR images to capture the whole luminosity range in a scene without loss of information into one final digital image.

INDEX OF PHOTOGRAPHERS

J.R.V.- Joseph R. Votano
K.H. - Karen Hosking;
K.S. - Karl Schanz
K.J. - Ken Jordan
R.L. - Robert Lamacq

INDEX OF LOCATIONS

PLATE	LOCATION	PHOTOGRAPHER
1	Clearwater, FL	K.H.
2	Agate Beach, OR	J.R.V.
3	Plum Island, Newburyport, MA	J.R.V.
4	Plum Island, Newburyport, MA	J.R.V.
5	St. Augustine Beach, St. Augustine, FL	J.R.V
6	St. Augustine Beach, St. Augustine, FL	J.R.V.
7	Jekyll Island, GA	J.R.V.
8	Sand Beach, Acadia Nat. Park, ME	J.R.V.
9	Hopewell, New Brunswick, Canada	J.R.V.
10	Mont St.-Michel, Normandy, France	J.R.V.
11	Lynn Shore Dr., Lynn, MA	K.H.
12	Bandon Beach, Bandon, OR	J.R.V.
13	Bandon Beach, Bandon, OR	J.R.V.
14	Bandon Beach, Bandon, OR	J.R.V.
15	Bandon Beach, Bandon, OR	J.R.V.
16	Face Rock, Bandon Beach, Bandon, OR	J.R.V.
17	Seal Rock, OR	J.R.V.
18	Ruby Beach, WA	J.R.V.
19	Hopewell Rocks, New Brunswick, Canada	J.R.V.
20	Good Harbor Beach, Gloucester, MA	J.R.V.
21	Cape Cod Nat. Seashore, MA	J.R.V.
22	Cape Cod Nat. Seashore, MA	J.R.V.
23	Prout's Neck, Cape Elizabeth, ME	J.R.V.
24	Wingaersheek Beach, Gloucester, MA	J.R.V.
25	Annisquam Light, Annisquam, MA	J.R.V.
26	Annisquam Light, Annisquam, MA	J.R.V.
27	Marsh hay, Atlantic St., Gloucester, MA	J.R.V.
28	Fall marsh hay, Atlantic St., Gloucester, MA	J.R.V.
29	Cordgrass, Atlantic St., Gloucester, MA	J.R.V.
30	Plum Island, Station 2, Newburyport. MA	J.R.V.
31	Plum Island, Station 2, Newburyport. MA	J.R.V.
32	San Juan, PR	J.R.V.
33	Plum Island, Station 1, Newburyport, MA	J.R.V.
34	Cape Cod Bay, Monomet, MA	J.R.V.
35	Plum Island, Station 1, Newburyport, MA	J.R.V.
36	Plum Island, Station 1, Newburyport, MA	J.R.V.
37	St. Augustine Beach, St. Augustine, FL	J.R.V.
38	York Beach, York, ME	J.R.V.
39	Plum Island, Station 1, Newburyport, MA	K.J.
40	Plum Island, Station 1, Newburyport, MA	K.J.
41	Plum Island, Station 1, Newburyport, MA	J.R.V.
42	Lynn Beach, Lynn, MA	J.R.V.
43	Duck Harbor Beach, Wellfleet, MA	J.R.V.
44	Near Cocoa Beach, FL	J.R.V.
45	Popham Beach, Popham, ME	J.R.V.
46	Salisbury State Park, Salisbury, MA	J.R.V.
47	Plum Island, Station 1, Newburyport, MA	K.J.
48	Otter Trail, Acadia Nat. Park, ME	J.R.V.
49	Pemaquid Point, Pemaquid, ME	J.R.V.
50	Bass Harbor Lighthouse, Acadia Nat. Park, ME	J.R.V.
51	Whitehead, Monhegan Island, ME	J.R.V.
52	Annisquam Lighthouse, Annisquam, MA	J.R.V.
53	Annisquam Lighthouse, Annisquam, MA	J.R.V.
54	Magnolia Coast, Magnolia, MA	J.R.V.

55	Rockport Beach, Rockport, MA	J.R.V.
56	Nahant's 40 Steps, Nahant, MA	J.R.V.
57	Tintagel, Cornwall, England	J.R.V.
58	Tintagel, Cornwall, England	J.R.V.
59	Cape Perpetua, OR	J.R.V.
60	Cape Perpetua, OR	J.R.V.
61	Cabot Trial, Nova Scotia	J.R.V.
62	Porthcurno Beach, West Cornwall, England	J.R.V.
63	Lost Coast Region, CA	J.R.V.
64	Cliffs of Moher, County Clare, Ireland	J.R.V.
65	Cliffs of Moher, County Clare, Ireland	J.R.V.
66	Bar Harbor, ME	J.R.V.
67	Trail Inlet, Acadia Nat. Park, ME	J.R.V.
68	New Harbor, ME	J.R.V.
69	New Harbor, ME	J.R.V.
70	New Harbor, ME	J.R.V.
71	Back Cove, New Harbor, ME	J.R.V.
72	The Sentinel, Back Cove, New Harbor, ME	J.R.V.
73	Old Friend, Back Cove, New Harbor, ME	J.R.V.
74	Old Friend, Back Cove, New Harbor, ME	J.R.V.
75	Old Friend, Back Cove, New Harbor, ME	J.R.V.
76	Thompson Pier, Back Cove New Harbor, ME	J.R.V.
77	Mackerel Cove, Bailey's Island, ME	J.R.V.
78	Mackerel Cove, Bailey's Island, ME	J.R.V.
79	East Chatham, Cape Cod, MA	J.R.V.
80	East Chatham, Cape Cod, MA	J.R.V.
81	Rockport Harbor, Rockport, MA	J.R.V.
82	Branscombe Harbor, Devon, England	J.R.V.
83	Branscombe Harbor, Devon, England	J.R.V.
84	Port Isaac, Cornwall, England	J.R.V.
85	Port Isaac, Cornwall, England	J.R.V.
86	Dartmouth, Devon, England	J.R.V.
87	Tintagel, Cornwall, England	J.R.V.
88	Peggy's Cove, Nova Scotia, Canada	J.R.V.
89	Peggy's Cove, Nova Scotia, Canada	J.R.V.
90	Annisquam Lighthouse, Annisquam, MA	J.R.V.
91	Annisquam Lighthouse, Annisquam, MA	J.R.V.
92	Annisquam Lighthouse, Annisquam, MA	J.R.V.
93	Pemaquid Lighthouse, Pemaquid, ME	K.S.
94	Pemaquid Lighthouse, Pemaquid, ME	J.R.V.
95	Pemaquid Lighthouse, Pemaquid, ME	J.R.V.
96	Ponce De Leon Lighthouse, Ponce Inlet, FL	J.R.V.
97	Ponce De Leon Lighthouse, Ponce Inlet, FL	J.R.V.
98	Stage Harbor Light, Chatham, MA	K.H.
99	Peggy's Cove Light, Nova Scotia, Canada	J.R.V.
100	Monhegan Light, Monhegan Island, ME	J.R.V.
101	Portland Lighthouse, Cape Elizabeth, ME	J.R.V.
102	Portland Lighthouse, Cape Elizabeth, ME	J.R.V.
103	Cape Blanco Lighthouse, Port Orford, OR	J.R.V.
104	Yaquina Head Lighthouse, OR	J.R.V.
105	St. Augustine Lighthouse, St. Augustine, FL	J.R.V.
106	Tybee Lighthouse, Tybee Island, GA	J.R.V.
107	Tybee Lighthouse, Tybee Island, GA	J.R.V.
108	Heceta Head Lighthouse, Florence, OR	J.R.V.
109	Nubble Light, York, ME	K.J.
110	Outside San Juan, Puerto Rico	J.R.V.

111	Beer-Branscombe, Devon, England	J.R.V.
112	Key West, FL	J.R.V.
113	Old Orchard Beach, ME	J.R.V.
114	St. Augustine Beach, St. Augustine, FL	J.R.V.
115	St. John's Pier, St. Augustine, FL	J.R.V.
116	Rt.1 to Key West, FL	J.R.V.
117	Monhegan Island, ME	J.R.V.
118	Monhegan Island, ME	J.R.V.
119	Clovelly, Cornwall, England	J.R.V.
120	Wingaersheek Beach, Gloucester, MA	J.R.V.
121	Fort Phoenix, Fairhaven, RI	J.R.V.
122	On the Road, New Brunswick, Canada	J.R.V.
123	St. Augustine Beach, St. Augustine, FL	J.R.V.
124	Clammers, Gloucester, MA	J.R.V.
125	Tidal Mill, Dinard, France	J.R.V.
126	Abandoned House, Rt. 337, Nova Scotia, Canada	J.R.V.
127	Manana Island, ME	J.R.V.
128	Salisbury Beach, Salisbury, MA	J.R.V.
129	Dartmouth Castle, Dartmouth, England	J.R.V.
130	Polperro, Cornwall, England	J.R.V.
131	Beach, Annisquam, MA	J.R.V.
132	Pemaquid Point, Pemaquid, ME	J.R.V.
133	Lonely Boat, Back Cove, New Harbor, ME	J.R.V.
134	Back Cove, New Harbor, ME	J.R.V.
135	The Friendship of Salem, Salem, MA	J.R.V.
136	Lunenburg, Nova Scotia	J.R.V.
137	Along Rt 333, Nova Scotia, Canada	J.R.V.
138	Along Rt 333, Nova Scotia, Canada	J.R.V.
139	Pemaquid Harbor, Pemaquid, ME	J.R.V.
140	Harbor at Monhegan Island, ME	J.R.V.
141	Harbor at New Harbor, ME	J.R.V.
142	Nahant Beach, Lynn Shore Drive, Lynn, MA	J.R.V.
143	Good Harbor Beach, Gloucester, MA	J.R.V.
144	Early Morning, Bar Harbor, ME	J.R.V.
145	Sunrise over Cape Cod Bay, MA	J.R.V.
146	Good Harbor Beach, Gloucester, MA	R.L.
147	Lobster Boat Heading Out, ME	J.R.V.
148	Setting Sun, Heceta Head, OR	J.R.V.
149	Moon over Cape Cod Bay, MA	J.R.V.
150	Rise of Supermoon, Cape Cod Bay, MA	J.R.V.
151	Montage, Supermoon over Cape Cod Bay, MA	J.R.V.